INGREDIENTS
FOR SUCCESS

10

BEST PRACTICES

FOR

BUSINESS

AND

LIFE

Ingredients for Success: 10 Best Practices for Business and Life

BY

Joseph James Slawek

kickstand
Books That Hold Up

DEDICATION

This book is dedicated to those people who discover the richness of God's Word and who seek His Kingdom in their daily life and work.

This book is dedicated to my wife, Mary, and our children, Luke, Megan, Elliana, Kirk, Mallory, and Joy as I am so privileged to call them my family.

TABLE OF CONTENTS

ACKNOWLEDGMENTS

I acknowledge Jesus as my Lord and Savior.

I am pleased to acknowledge Dr. Charles Haley who came into my life as an "angel" and who began to reveal God's Word to me as it applies to everyday life and work.

I acknowledge my gifted writing partner, Bill Butterworth, who kept me on track in completing this first book.

I acknowledge Crown Ministries and all the other workplace and business ministries who kept me fascinated with the Word of God.

Thank you to Debbie Mast for her tireless work on project management and coordinating all the many pieces of this project.

Thank you to Keri Wyatt Kent and Julie Busteed of Kickstand Books for their writing and editing assistance.

I acknowledge Matthew 25 as the source of timeless principles; first, for our entire lives and secondly, for our businesses.

INTRODUCTION
THE 10 BEST PRACTICES FOR SUCCESS

Growing up, I went to church on Sundays. My interactions with God were meaningful, but they stopped as I walked out the door of the church, and didn't resume until the following Sunday.

So when a dedicated Christian businessman told me, "God has something to say about business," I was surprised, but also delighted.

When I first heard that statement, back in 1988, you could not have said anything else that would have gotten me more deeply into the Bible. I came to the scriptures with an open and curious mind because I knew either the Bible was true all the time and everywhere I went, or the opposite—it was not true anytime or anywhere I went. I realized that God had business strategies that worked, and he also had a desire to help me succeed.

Once I began studying God's Word, I realized that within it are biblical principles that provide insight to all of us in the marketplace. What's more, beyond the fact that they are all true, these principles have three characteristics in common:

- They are predictable.
- They are universal.
- They are trustworthy.

As I continued to read the Bible, I also read some wonderful Christian writers on this subject. I will mention their names and books later, but for now, suffice it to say that I was soaking up all the knowledge my brain could absorb. For a guy who had been brought up only knowing God from a church pew, this proved to be an extraordinary time in my life as I began to know God from my desk view.

In the fields of business, law, medicine, and elsewhere, people talk about the "best practices" as a way of describing the highest standards of innovation, the most reliable and current ways of doing whatever they do.

God has best practices, too, for business and for life. He has something to say about how we conduct our daily lives—which for most of us means the way we operate in the marketplace. He has strategies for success in business and life.

I'm now CEO of FONA Inc., a multi-national company that creates flavorings for the food and beverage and pharmaceutical industries. I know that quality flavorings require quality ingredients. And success requires quality "ingredients" as well. That's what this book is about.

Whether you are a clerk or a CEO, you are called to lead. You may lead only one other person. You may have to put leadership principles to work on a team of which you are a part. But if you use these best practices, you'll not only find success, but you'll also know that you are living according to God's Word. That obedience is a reward in itself.

Focusing on Matthew 25

Many of the scriptures that I read and studied were relevant to my everyday business model, but I found myself repeatedly attracted to the parables and the sayings of Jesus recorded in Matthew 25. The Lord Jesus used parables as teaching tools—some scholars have referred to the parables as "windows that let the light in"— stories that illuminate the truth. The chapter contains three sections: The Parable of the Ten Virgins, The Parable of the Talents, and the teaching on The Sheep and the Goats. All of the words in those verses spoke to me mightily about the way I was conducting my life and my business.

In fact, these verses changed the way I did business–and life. From the wisdom in this chapter, I gleaned ten principles, or best practices. This book is about those practices, and how to apply them to both your business and personal life.

Before I share these ten practices, ten ingredients for success, let's take a look at the passage they came from. This brilliant teaching of Jesus is as relevant today as it was when he first offered it to people 2,000 years ago. Don't be in a hurry to power through these words—take your time and read carefully. And as you learn the ten practices, you may want to revisit the text to read each section again.

The Parable of the Ten Virgins

At that time the kingdom of heaven will be like ten virgins who took their lamps and went out to meet the bridegroom. Five of them were foolish and five were wise. The foolish ones took their lamps but did not take any oil with them. The wise ones, however, took oil in jars along with their lamps. The bridegroom was a long time in coming, and they all became drowsy and fell asleep.

At midnight the cry rang out: "Here's the bridegroom! Come out to meet him!"

Then all the virgins woke up and trimmed their lamps. The foolish ones said to the wise, "Give us some of your oil; our lamps are going out."

"No," they replied, "there may not be enough for both us and you.

3

Instead, go to those who sell oil and buy some for yourselves."

But while they were on their way to buy the oil, the bridegroom arrived. The virgins who were ready went in with him to the wedding banquet. And the door was shut.

Later the others also came. "Lord, Lord," they said, "open the door for us!"

But he replied, "Truly I tell you, I don't know you."

Therefore keep watch, because you do not know the day or the hour.

—*Matthew 25:1-13 (NIV)*

The Parable of the Bags of Gold

Again, it will be like a man going on a journey, who called his servants and entrusted his wealth to them. To one he gave five bags of gold, to another two bags, and to another one bag, each according to his ability. Then he went on his journey. The man who had received five bags of gold went at once and put his money to work and gained five bags more. So also, the one with two bags of gold gained two more. But the man who had received one bag went off, dug a hole in the ground and hid his master's money.

After a long time the master of those servants returned and settled accounts with them. The man who had received five bags of gold brought the other five. "Master," he said, "you entrusted me with five bags of gold. See, I have gained five more."

His master replied, "Well done, good and faithful servant! You have been faithful with a few things; I will put you in charge of many things. Come and share your master's happiness!"

The man with two bags of gold also came. "Master," he said, "you entrusted me with two bags of gold; see, I have gained two more."

His master replied, "Well done, good and faithful servant! You have been faithful with a few things; I will put you in charge of many things. Come and share your master's happiness!"

Then the man who had received one bag of gold came. "Master," he said, "I knew that you are a hard man, harvesting where you have not sown and gathering where you have not scattered seed. So I was afraid and went out and hid your gold in the ground. See, here is what belongs to you."

His master replied, "You wicked, lazy servant! So you knew that I harvest where I have not sown and gather where I have not scattered seed? Well then, you should have put my money on deposit with bankers, so that when I returned I would have received it back with interest.

"So take the bag of gold from him and give it to the one who has ten bags. For whoever has will be given more, and they will have an abundance. Whoever does not have, even what they have will be taken from them. And throw that worthless servant outside, into the darkness, where there will be weeping and gnashing of teeth."

—*Matthew 25:14-30 (NIV)*

The Sheep and the Goats

When the Son of Man comes in his glory, and all the angels with him, he will sit on his glorious throne. All the nations will be gathered before him, and he will separate the people one from another as a shepherd separates the sheep from the goats. He will put the sheep on his right and the goats on his left.

Then the King will say to those on his right, "Come, you who

are blessed by my Father; take your inheritance, the kingdom prepared for you since the creation of the world. For I was hungry and you gave me something to eat, I was thirsty and you gave me something to drink, I was a stranger and you invited me in, I needed clothes and you clothed me, I was sick and you looked after me, I was in prison and you came to visit me."

Then the righteous will answer him, "Lord, when did we see you hungry and feed you, or thirsty and give you something to drink? When did we see you a stranger and invite you in, or needing clothes and clothe you? When did we see you sick or in prison and go to visit you?"

The King will reply, "Truly I tell you, whatever you did for one of the least of these brothers and sisters of mine, you did for me."

Then he will say to those on his left, "Depart from me, you who are cursed, into the eternal fire prepared for the devil and his angels. For I was hungry and you gave me nothing to eat, I was thirsty and you gave me nothing to drink, I was a stranger and you did not invite me in, I needed clothes and you did not clothe me, I was sick and in prison and you did not look after me."

They also will answer, "Lord, when did we see you hungry or thirsty or a stranger or needing clothes or sick or in prison, and did not help you?"

He will reply, "Truly I tell you, whatever you did not do for one of the least of these, you did not do for me."

Then they will go away to eternal punishment, but the righteous to eternal life.

—*Matthew 25:31-46 (NIV)*

Ten Best Practices

There are so many lessons about life and business that we can draw from this chapter. But I've dipped into this well of truth and drawn just ten best practices—God's best practices for business and life. If you do these things, you'll begin to see your work differently, you'll find the purpose in what you're doing, and I believe God, who loves to reward his faithful servants generously, will bless you.

Here are the ten practices we will be unpacking in the pages that follow:

1. **Boldly, yet compassionately, tell the truth.** We must tell the truth in order to define reality and fight denial. Truth-telling is an essential practice for anyone at any level of any organization.

2. **Plan ahead but be ready for surprises.** We are responsible for planning and preparation, and also for responding to surprises or crises.

3. **Know, develop, and use your unique abilities.** God assigns to each of us a certain amount of specific talents, gifts, resources, and abilities along with a unique personality, and the responsibility to use them.

4. **Use your talents responsibly or you'll lose them.** We are entrusted with God's resources in the form of our talents, skills, abilities, gifts, resources, etc. We have a responsibility to use them or lose them.

5. **Be ready for the accounting.** There is **always** an accounting—daily, weekly, monthly, annually. And eventually, there will be a final accounting from God—an external audit of your life and

what you did with your talents. There is always an accounting.

6. **Invest your talents faithfully for maximum return.** We will all get the same reward from our master if we use our respective talents properly. He will say, "Well done, good and faithful servant."

7. **Aim for excellence, not perfection.** There are only four outcomes at home or at work: failure, mediocrity, excellence, or perfection. Excellence is our target because it requires and motivates us to get better.

8. **Be strong and courageous.** Fear, though a normal part of life, can cause us to bury our talents. Fear and perfectionism both create procrastination.

9. **Redistribute unused talents and resources.** Unused gifts, resources, and talents are always recycled to someone who will use them faithfully. When we don't use our gifts, they'll be given to someone else.

10. **Express gratitude to God and others.** Gratitude is our first priority and it precedes all rewards.

We will take a full chapter to unwrap each best practice, each ingredient for success, so that you'll be able to apply them to your own life and business. When we do business God's way, he will bless our efforts and prosper us. But the essential foundation for all ten practices is living with integrity. It's all about becoming and then being **trustworthy**. If that's not there, all the practices in the world won't help. So let's look at what the Bible has to say about how we can have success in business and in life.

Chapter One
Boldly, yet Compassionately, Tell the Truth

We must tell the truth in order to define reality and fight denial. Truth-telling is an essential practice for anyone at any level of any organization.

While all people are created in the image of God and have equal value, they do not all have equal abilities. This is a truth that is clear from the parables in Matthew 25. There are wise virgins and foolish virgins. Some servants can be entrusted with five bags of gold, others with only one, because they have differing abilities. This may feel a bit harsh, but it is truth— presented clearly in Scripture and further evidenced by our experience in life.

Talents are not equally distributed. If 100 people start a ten-mile race, their talents, giftedness, preparations, sportsmanship all become evident.

Similarly, Matthew 25 talks about the elements of preparation, individual talents, giftedness, and sportsmanship. We are entrusted by our Creator with certain gifts and talents, which we are required to grow. He puts them on loan to us, and we have our choice to develop them, use them, or lose them. I think that is exactly why Matthew 25 is so applicable to business.

The reality then, in the marketplace, and in life, is that we live in a world in which we are designed to serve others, and that requires planning and preparation and the use of individual gifts and talents. This is the reality in which a Christian business person operates. The parables of Matthew 25 are true, and they remind us the importance of telling the truth in order to define reality and help those we lead or work beside to fight denial so that they can thrive.

As a leader, it is my job to define reality, fight denial, see patterns, and predict the future. It begins with defining reality for my company. There are both internal and external realities as well as natural numbness, disbelief, and denial to these internal and external realities. As patterns begin to emerge, the leader can predict the future, not in a prophetic sense but certainly in the sense of extending the pattern to its natural conclusion.

The above principle may seem simplistic at first, but a more careful study uncovers the fact that this little phrase represents one of the most concise, yet cogent definitions of a leader that you may ever read. In those three aspects, you can see the entire scope of a leader's responsibility. It's not based on an ivory tower, academic, not-of-this-world way of thinking, either. It is firmly based on reality. And that's a great place to begin our study together.

The Principle Found in Matthew 25

It is very important to understand from the outset that this collection of ten best practices is not a concoction of my own thinking, but rather these are concepts that come from the Bible, God's Word; therefore, it is beyond a man's opinion, and more than a personal passion. It is the God of the universe speaking personally and profoundly to each and every one of us. That should send a shiver up our spines!

We will link each principle to the words, phrases, or concepts found specifically in Matthew 25 as they relate to each topic. As we begin this journey, however, I wanted to start with the practice of truth-telling and defining reality as number one because it is really the foundation of all we will study together. What do I mean when I say that? I feel it is essential for each of us to firmly grasp two overarching concepts about the Bible:

- Matthew 25 in its entirety is 100 percent *TRUTH*.
- It is in that truth that we find *REALITY*.

The parables and teachings in Matthew 25, and throughout Scripture, are all God's truth, preserved for us through the centuries so we could learn and grow from their lessons. Sometimes it is not possible to teach something easily. Parables require us to wrestle with the truth, to dig it out. The Lord uses this struggle with the truth to drive us to his Word. It is that truth that provides the basis for what is real. A business person has no place in the business world if he or she isn't firmly established and well-grounded in reality. It's the leader's primary function and the first part of our principle—defining reality.

As a CEO, this translates into my ability to first imagine and then articulate our vision, our mission, and our values. Here's how this fleshes out in the reality of running a business.

I started Flavors of North America (now called FONA) because I wanted to put these principles into practice. After 26 years in business, these principles have guided us toward success—and not just success as measured by the bottom line.

Our growth has been solid and steady as we've expanded from a local company to an international one. But we've also received the recognition of our peers—not just for our business success, but also for the culture we've created.

In 2012, after being named one of Chicago's 101 Best & Brightest

Companies to Work For, for the seventh year in a row, we went on to the national level and were presented with the top award for mid-size businesses. We've been recognized by *Inc.* magazine for six years running as one of the fastest growing private companies in the country, and also as Manufacturer of the Year by the Safe Quality Food Institute (SQFI). In 1999, I was inducted into the Chicago Area Entrepreneurship Hall of Fame. In 2011, I was named Ernst & Young Entrepreneur of the Year® for Manufacturing in the Midwest—an honor that surprised and humbled me—and for which I give glory to God.

The company that started with ideas sketched on napkins during meals with my business partners has grown—doubling its revenues every four years—mostly by applying the principles I'm going to share with you. These concepts permeate our culture and everything we do at FONA.

As the leader of this organization, I need to communicate reality. Each day, I have to remind the people who work with me of our vision, mission and values—and help them figure out how to live those out in their daily work.

Most companies share their vision, mission, and values with employees when they are first hired—and FONA is no exception to that rule. But even my most dedicated employees may not sit down and read those documents every morning before work—so part of my role is to remind them not only of what we believe in, but also how we live it out. In other words, to provide truth—define reality.

It is vital for employees to catch that vision and plug into the same reality. Everyone needs to know where the organization is going and work together to move it forward. Otherwise it will be like paddling a canoe in opposite directions and getting nowhere!

We've very carefully crafted vision, mission, and values statements, which we share with our employees. (See Appendix A.) We also post key concepts from those values on the walls around our company headquarters, just to keep them regularly in front of people.

A company's vision articulates where the company is going—its ongoing goals and top priorities. Its mission tells how that vision will be achieved.

FONA has become a leader in the flavor industry. That market position has come from our highest values, which are GROWTH and EXCELLENCE. The relentless pursuit of excellence translates to customer growth, employee growth, and business growth. It drives us to be innovators. But innovation without excellence is just moving quickly in the wrong direction. The reality I must constantly remind our employees of is this: excellence matters, and it flows out of their small, daily actions and decisions.

Our company creates flavorings for the food and beverage industry, and the pharmaceutical industry. Your company might do something completely different—and your values might be different as well. But it's essential that you figure out where you are going, and keep that mission in front of everyone on your team.

For example, at FONA, we're not just selling to our customers. We're trying to support them and help them succeed because their success means our success. That's a reality that I have to repeat often.

But just talking about vision and mission is not enough to ensure success. It's essential that we use the best management practices and processes that we can. We hire and develop world-class talent, and offer highly competitive compensation to keep those people on our team. This winning approach fuels our consistent high growth and creates the profitability necessary to fund our continued expansion.

The Truth Sometimes Hurts

While I love to talk about the great things that are going on here, boldly telling the truth sometimes means I must talk about things that need to be corrected as well.

For example, there have been occasions in our product lines, where one of our business units, despite our best efforts, despite continual growing investment, did not perform well.

Because it is the leader's job to define reality, fight denial, see the pattern, and from that pattern predict the future, I needed to make a decision. It is in those cases that business units or product lines have been dropped. Using this formula we have adopted or dropped business units and products lines that have failed to perform over a reasonable time.

This gets more difficult, but is just as essential, when you have to apply the same standards to your people. There have been times when defining reality for a sales person, for example, has been difficult and painful. The person may be well-liked and fit in well, but he or she just isn't able to achieve the results we are called to in Matthew 25. Personnel issues, with poor performance, are perhaps the most difficult place to define reality, but it remains our job to define reality, fight denial, see patterns and predict the future.

After a reasonable amount of time, there is always the CEO's dilemma: do I continue to invest resources in a person, a territory, a business unit, an investment, when the reality is that there has been no return on investment?

As well-liked as that person or project may be, it is denial to say that anything is going to change, and I must accept the pattern that predicts the future from the patterns I see.

The Values at FONA

When I started FONA, my team and I set out to create a culture that is partner-centered, growth-oriented, positive, and dynamic. We attract employees who are willing, able, and committed to personal and professional growth. Our belief is that all people have innate value and significance and are worthy of dignity and respect. We seek to create and sustain an open environment that is palpably inclusive, values diversity, promotes innovation, and provides growth opportunities for ALL FONA team members. We are committed to the highest standards of ethical and moral conduct as we manage and grow our business. We run our business according to the truths of the Bible, even though we are certainly a "secular" company. Our employees are diverse in their backgrounds and beliefs, but they come to join our team knowing that we care about them, but also that we care about values like doing the right thing, stewarding our resources well, and being generous.

In fact, one way we reminded ourselves of that reality was when we built our new building in Geneva, Illinois. As we built this beautiful factory and office headquarters, we placed our oldest, used Bibles in the foundation of the building and located them under the key offices, conference rooms, and areas and in every entrance to the building. The reality we wanted to remember is that all things are built on the Word of God.

For example, doing the right thing means being "family friendly." While many companies claim that, do they actually do it in reality? We have a room set aside for moms who are just returning from maternity leave. Their babies' caregivers can bring the children to this room, and our employees can visit with them during their breaks. Nursing moms can have a chance to be with their child during a lunch or other break. That, to us, seemed like doing the right thing for everyone involved. It wasn't the cheapest option or the easiest, but it was the right one.

As a company that provides flavors for food, beverages, and medicines, we are subject to government regulations. Doing the right thing in this area means exceeding compliance levels for all regulatory agencies and cooperating with them fully. We don't cut corners, instead choosing to go above the standard. It's not cheaper, but it's a wise investment, and it's another way we do the right thing in all situations.

Another value I believe every company should have, and one we have high on our list at FONA, is to "demonstrate a relentless, passionate partner-centricity." Because the words we choose to cast a vision for our team will shape the way they see reality, we refer to companies who purchase our products and services as partners, rather than just customers.

Our business model is built around finding compelling, unique solutions for our partners' greatest business challenges. We believe there is an important distinction between customers and partners. Customers look for concrete selection criteria which can be objectified and researched; partners seek mutually-beneficial, long-term relationships based on trust and solutions well beyond the simple criteria.

The reality that I must continually remind our team to focus on is this: We are entrepreneurial, passionate, and focused in delighting our partners. We believe that all parties make an impact on our business success. We over-invest to understand partner needs. We have and will deliberately build reserve capacity to meet unspoken demand, and thus, are ready for our partners to succeed with us. We listen for our partner feedback, and we act upon their insights.

Here at FONA, the reality is that we are striving every day to put these resources to work in a practical manner. Not to do so would be denying what we are brought together to do and it is fighting that denial that represents another part of the leader's job description. Once reality is defined, it can be easily overlooked or denied, and it's my job to fight the denial. This situation can often be seen as a "blind spot," either of an employee or of the whole company. It's not that there is intentional denial of reality, it's more of a "lack of awareness" at the time. That's where I can come alongside and gently help them see the truth. It's the CEO at work in a very personal way. I serve as the human reminder of the reality of the company and of the marketplace which we serve.

It stands to reason that if I am defining reality and fighting denial, I am going to be telling the truth. Honesty is the best policy but it is not always the easiest, the most convenient, or the most popular. Telling the truth can cause the CEO to be perceived as a "tough guy" without a full compassionate awareness of his employee's specific situation. Those that know me know that I work very hard at being a kind, caring leader. But that *never* means skimping on the truth.

The Lord Jesus told us: "And you shall know the truth and the truth will set you free" (John 8:32, NIV).

There's reality for you! That's the Truth, dear reader. Don't deny it. Embrace it.

CHAPTER TWO
PLAN AHEAD BUT BE READY
FOR SURPRISES

We are responsible for planning and preparation, and also for responding to surprises or crises.

O nce we are grounded in the reality of the truth of all of God's Word, we can begin focusing our attention on the best practices that we can learn from God's Word. So after we tell the truth, we have to act on that truth. We need to plan ahead, but also to remember that things don't always go as planned. So we anticipate what we think will happen, prepare for that, but we also prepare for things to go awry. Let's look at the particular passage from which these principles flow.

The Principle Found in Matthew 25

The first of the three parables recorded in Matthew's text tells the story of ten virgins who were invited to a wedding. They grabbed their lamps and went out to meet the *bridegroom.* This was a very significant, one-time assignment. Unlike Western weddings, it is the bridegroom who receives most of the attention in ancient Middle Eastern weddings, not the bride. So, the virgins must have been excited about their potential meeting with the star of the show! Yet, something truly unfortunate happened. Only five of the ten virgins remembered to bring oil for the lamps. The other five came unprepared for the use of their lamps. A little planning and preparation would have solved their problem, if they had taken the time necessary to think the entire process through to its conclusion. They did not plan ahead and anticipate properly, and as a result, they were not ready.

We know that we in our Christian lives eagerly await Jesus' return. This parable of the ten virgins reminds us of that truth, and exhorts us to be ready at all times. But there is also an application to our business lives.

The five virgins who ended up being described as "foolish" missed their assignments. This was a one-time opportunity. In a modern-day analogy, it was like remembering to bring their flashlights, but forgetting to bring their batteries! In the world of business, this principle addresses the concept of employee engagement. What do my employees bring to the workplace that indicates they are truly prepared for the work at hand?

This may sound like a silly illustration, but imagine someone in your life who continually complains to you about the clothes he or she is wearing, saying, "I hate the way I look in this shirt!" or "This suit makes me look bad, doesn't it?" or "This is an ugly necktie, I can't believe I am wearing it!" After hearing just about all you can stand, you want to answer back to this person, "Well, who dressed you?"

It is important for me to understand that I am responsible for the resources and opportunities I have been given. It is up to me to *plan* out carefully and strategically how my resources will be best used. If I don't like how I am dressed, I alone am responsible to make the change. I may dress quickly in the dark, so I need to modify my plan! Setting the alarm a few minutes earlier might help. Or perhaps it means laying out my clothes the night before while I have the opportunity to do it with the assistance of the light.

Whether you are a new recruit at the bottom of the ladder or the

CEO, what do you need to do each day to come to work prepared? What thinking do you need to engage in, so that you can anticipate potential problems and be ready to overcome them?

In the world of Bible times, a wedding was the "Big Event" in a person's life. It would only happen once and it was the "opportunity of a lifetime." The five foolish virgins missed the boat by not seizing it in the "lifetime of the opportunity" and that's why they were considered foolish. They truly lost out because of their inability to engage in the best practice of preparation with the resources they had been given.

Life Lessons in Planning Ahead

Planning and preparation are not just for young women in the first century Holy Land. I learned about this principle at a very early age. I was eight years old, growing up on the northwest side of Chicago when I had my first glimpse of what I could do with the resources that I had been given. From my earliest recollection I was taught by my parents the importance of hard work, so it should come as no surprise that I was already a part of the workforce at the age of eight. I was a paper boy, faithfully delivering the afternoon paper, *The Chicago Daily News* every day. As the oldest child in the Slawek family, I was responsible to see that I earned some of my own money. I took the responsibility seriously.

Eight years old is a bit young to be throwing papers, but I got along just fine—with one major exception. Part of my route included a three-story apartment building that required me to get the paper delivered to each family on their first, second, or third floor balcony. The first and second story created no problems, even for a youngster like me. I could throw those newspapers onto their balconies in perfect position.

But the third floor was where the challenge presented itself.

Try as I might, I just couldn't get those newspapers to land on the desired third- floor balconies. I was only eight, and part of the dilemma rested in the truth that I simply wasn't strong enough to throw a paper that high with any degree of accuracy. Let's just say that early on, I did a lot of extra throwing in order to get those papers to their desired location. It was frustrating at first, but I learned persistence and discipline. I also learned how to **plan and prepare** for that particular hurdle. I knew those third-story balconies were going to require additional time, in comparison to throwing the other papers, and I adjusted accordingly. Being prepared allowed me more time to 'practice.' Before too long, I was a pro at third-story launches. What a feeling of accomplishment!

Planning Ahead Today

I will fill in the missing twenty-year gap in the next chapter, but I want to fast- forward two decades in order to illustrate how I needed planning and preparation in my life as I approached one of the biggest steps of my business journey.

Early in my thirties, I found myself as the highest compensated sales person at Food Materials, a flavor company I had worked in since the time I was in high school, including during my college years. Through the effective use of planning and preparation, I had worked hard at learning everything I could about our customers' needs and consequently, I rose through the company. Ultimately I became the assistant to the president, which became part of how I prepared to lead my own company (even though I didn't know it at time), because I got to observe what a CEO must deal with on a daily basis.

And, it was becoming abundantly clear that based on what I

had learned early and in my sales career, I enjoyed autonomy. Knowing yourself, your strengths, and your temperament can help you to be prepared. It will shape your goals.

As I continued to plan for my future, I experienced an ever-increasing desire for autonomy. It is not uncommon for men to go through that sort of phase, especially in their early to mid-thirties. The more I pondered that desire, the more I sought counsel from those I respected, and the more I prayed for God's guidance, the more the same thought kept reverberating over and over in my brain: If I really want autonomy, I need to have my own business!

I was becoming so successful at Food Materials that I found coworkers began cheering for my downfall, or at least a reduced compensation package. As you can imagine, it's a frustrating position to be in when your own management peers look for ways to reduce your compensation. If I started my own company, my performance would never be my own enemy. Just the opposite, it would lend great credence to guaranteeing my own success.

At the same time that I was experiencing growing frustration with the values of my peers at Food Materials, I also experienced a growing awareness and interest in my spiritual life. For the first time in my life I was fully realizing the opening sentence I wrote in this book: God cares about my business. I knew Food Materials wasn't my company and therefore its owner could do with it whatever he wanted to do, with or without my input. If I thought there was a better way to do it, I needed to do it that way—by starting my own company.

But starting a company requires planning and preparation. So before I could begin, I needed to prepare by putting together a strong team. I had a partner, Bill Bowring, who was going to run the sales department, so he and I began brainstorming all the aspects of creating a new company. I knew if I was going to start a company, I needed a good plan. Once again, I was truly grateful to be the assistant to the president for those years at Food Materials, since that position required me to be on multiple planning committees, providing me a close-up view of what planning and preparation are all about. I also had the opportunity to be mentored by that president, Arthur T. Schramm, who taught me about the industry and about what's involved in being the president of a company. I also saw that God had given me exposure to the entire operations of a flavor company.

We first put together a sales and marketing plan, which was no problem at all, since we both had such strong backgrounds in those areas. Then we turned our attention to the financial plan, which was significantly more difficult, but we were able to cobble together some figures that made sense. Finally, we put together a manufacturing and technical plan that helped us see we needed our industry friend Leslie Fisher as one of our first hires, in order to have a technical leader for our laboratory. We also added T.J. Widuch as our go-to guy for customer service and operations. The four of us made up the original four at FONA. Leslie, T.J., Bill, and I would live or die off how effectively we could translate our plans into reality.

Since FONA was planned while I worked for a different company and owed that company the obligation of an honest day's work, plans for the new company, our entrepreneurial effort, were done on our own time, perhaps during a breakfast, lunch, or dinner. So many of our ideas were not on computerized spread sheets, but rather sketched on paper napkins we'd grab as we began to discuss the big ideas, the next steps, and the sequence of things we had to find out and learn.

These were most often in the form of the vision for the company. We were planning ahead by asking ourselves to get clear about our vision. Nature, people, and technology were key elements in our vision. *Nature* as the model for great flavors, *people* as the artist creating and delivering those great flavors, and *technology* as the means to extend our competitive advantage as a method.

Our plans (we still have many of those napkins with sketches on them) often took the form of questions: How do we _____? (incorporate, hire an accountant, hire an attorney . . .) A great number of them were checklists in the way of next steps.

In April of 1987, we pulled the trigger. I've often said in retrospect that pulling the trigger is the most difficult part of the entire process. One can dream, one can hope, one can pray, one can plan, but when it's go-time, there really are only a select few with the one-time surge of courage necessary to go all the way in the process. "Thinking of being in business for yourself" is very different than "Being in business for yourself."

Implement a Planning Process

A key part of business leadership at any level is strategic planning. Rather than simply responding to the crisis of the moment, we need a process in place that will allow us to stay on task with our goals.

It's obvious from the parables in Matthew 25 that planning is essential. But that truth is not enough; we need to know *how* to plan, not just that we ought to do it. I believe there are four key principles for effective strategic planning. They are as follows:

1. **Strategize in three key areas.** It is logically impossible for everything to be your top priority, but a lot of leaders try to run their business this way. I recommend that strategy be focused on these three areas: a go-to-market plan (how our goods and services get to the people who need them); a people plan (managing our human resources); and a financial plan. Everything else in your business should flow from those three key areas.

2. **Follow the natural order.** These three areas have a logical sequence. Start with your customers (without them, you don't have a business) and how you get your product or service to them. Then, move on to your people plan—how you will train and equip them to deliver what your customers need. Once you know the objectives for the first two, you can make financial plans that support the first two areas. (Many business leaders get this backward, and start with the bottom line, which might seem logical but always backfires).

3. **Set goals for three time periods.** Think about what your goals for your company are for the next year, the next three years, and the next ten years. Obviously, your strategic plan for the coming year will have much more detail about specific activities that will move you toward your objectives. The three-year-plan will be more about results you want to achieve. The plan for the next decade, of course, will be more visionary—where you want to be and how will you get there.

4. **Create a calendar** with those time periods and their specific goals. Clearly communicate those goals, and their deadlines, across the organization.

As you engage in planning and preparation, don't get so focused on the goals and the tasks that you forget about the people who are helping you implement those goals. Take time to encourage your people, to tell them when they have done a good job, and that you appreciate it. A little encouragement and gratitude goes a long way toward motivating your team to do their best.

The last thing I want to do is give the impression that as long as you plan and prepare, you will not encounter problems and only experience success. No, my friend, nothing could be further from the truth. At FONA we met and dealt with daily problems punctuated by occasional crises from its earliest days in 1987, all the way to the most recent of times. But our Lord has been faithful and continues to be so. We will talk more about crisis in later chapters.

The Lord Jesus gave us this wonderful metaphor about our service to Him, as recorded by Luke in his gospel:

> If you do not carry your own cross and follow me, you cannot be my disciple.
>
> But don't begin until you **count the cost.** For who would begin construction of a building without first calculating the cost to see if there is enough money to finish it? Otherwise you might complete only the foundation before running out of money, and then everyone would laugh at you. They would say, "There's the person who started that building and couldn't afford to finish it!."
>
> —Luke 14:27-30 (NLT, emphasis added)

"Count the cost"—that's planning! Planning and preparation are absolutely vital to the success of your business, just as they are absolutely essential to the success in every other aspect of your life. Take the words of our Lord, seriously, my friend. He has your best interest at heart.

CHAPTER THREE
KNOW, DEVELOP, AND
USE YOUR UNIQUE ABILITIES

God assigns to each of us a certain amount of specific talents, gifts, resources, and abilities along with a unique personality, and the responsibility to use them.

During a recent FONA leadership team retreat, our facilitator helped us work through a variety of exercises. One of the specific assignments was to identify the foundational resources we currently have in place. To assist us in our thinking, we were given seven different categories within the topic.

I love exercises of this nature, so I got right down to it. Resources like the ones I listed are our business "talents," entrusted to our call by God. The best practice of assessing your talents begins with an inventory like this. You may have to take some time away from the office to give this careful thought. Here are some of the answers I was able to articulate about our business.

You can do this whether you lead a company, a department, a small team, or even your family. What are the resources God has given you to use? For FONA, I came up with this list:

Physical Resources

- A World-class Facility
- Reserve Manufacturing Capacity
- Beautiful Campus
- Great Technical Equipment

- Great Midwestern Location
- Inventory
- Community

People Resources

- Great People
- Great Educational Backgrounds
- Great Culture
- Great Families
- Great Developers
- Great Competency

Intellectual Resources

- Technology and Innovation
- Flavor University®
- Intellectual Properties
- High Leadership IQ
- Previous Experiences
- Ability to Overcome
- Patents
- Trade Secrets
- Problem Solvers

Financial Resources

- Declining and Low Levels of Debt
- Borrowing Availability
- Great Relationships with Bankers

- Real Estate Values
- Facilities Value
- Inventories and Receivables
- Stable Purchase Patterns
- Great Customer Credit

Partner Resources

- Legal Partners
- Accounting Partners
- Community Partners
- C-level Leadership Partners
- Partner Level Customers
- Consulting Partners

Relational Resources

- Board of Advisors
- Slawek Family
- Our People's Families
- Industry Relationships
- Community Relationships
- Advisor and Auditor Relationships

Other Resources

- Good Name and Great Reputation
- Great Brand
- Culture
- Goodwill

• Healthy EQ Management

That list amazed me, and humbled me. God had entrusted so many resources to me, and to our company. And he expected me to use them. But knowing what the resources are is a critical first step.

The foolish servant buried his gold in the ground—an action with dire consequences. But just as devastating is the mistake many others make: they never unearth the gold, the talents, that lie within them in the first place. Imagine that you inherit a box of your grandmother's old things. You throw it in the attic and never even open it—assuming there's nothing of value in there. Years later, you find out that the box contained precious antique gold jewelry, worth more than you ever thought. You'd feel foolish and regretful when you figured out what was in the box, right? But not taking the time to figure out what skills and resources you've been given is just like storing a box of treasures in the attic, unopened.

The very idea of investment is future-oriented. What return will your investment bring? You have to assess your own talents, and use them for the maximum return. If you lead a company or a team, you are responsible not only for your own talents, but also for those of the people you lead. In Jesus' parable, each servant was given a certain number of bags of gold. Your people are part of your bag of gold.

A key value at FONA is investing in growth and innovation. We're future-oriented, believing that "our best work is ahead of us." In order for this to actually happen, we have to be willing to encourage experimentation (and thus accept setbacks and failure), and to invest in our people to stimulate growth and innovation. We take feedback seriously, and we examine our problems realistically and build capabilities and capacities to address our weaknesses. We establish structures and practices that encourage people to provide feedback to each other and invest in one another.

All of us have abilities. We see them as talents, skills, gifts, resources, etc. The point is that every person has talent, so what will you do with the talent you've been given?

The Principle Found in Matthew 25

You will recall from the parable of the talents in Matthew 25 that the three servants were each given different amounts of gold. The text uses the phrase, "each according to his ability," signifying this beautiful Biblical truth: all gifts and all people are important to God, yet God equips each of us differently, some more than others.

I would summarize Jesus' teaching this way: there are five-talent people, two-talent people and one-talent people. It would stand to reason that five-talent people can handle more than two-talent people and that one-talent people would be characterized as those who *fail* to do anything with what they've been given. One-talent people do not engage in the best practice of assessing their talents and using them.

So let's begin with assessment. How do you determine if you are a five-talent person, a two-talent person or a one-talent person? I believe it begins by taking a good look at who you are. Finding your own unique set of talents becomes the name of the game. As Jeff Caliguire states it:

Contrary to what you may have heard, you can't do anything you want. However, you can do what you were uniquely created to do.

When you accept your own uniqueness and quit trying to

be something or someone you were never intended to be, you are liberated. No matter how lucrative, prestigious, or available other things appear, they are just trappings, because the exclusively unique you is best. By fully accepting and engaging who you were meant to be, you find freedom. You live in your own skin. You let your life speak. Live your own life, not someone else's or something less.[1]

Whether we are gifted in sports, business, cooking, teaching, studying, or sewing—we each have the responsibility to apply and to grow our talents according to our abilities. We all have unique gifts, and we're all on our way to being somewhere else.

Becoming a Two-Talent President

When I first began to study this passage and try to apply it to my own life, I took a long, hard look at my gifts as a CEO and quickly came to the conclusion that I was not a five-talent president. The five-talent crew is made up of the men and women who do things like running the large companies whose stocks are traded on Wall Street. Thus, my only other two choices were to be a two-talent president or a one-talent failure. That made the choice a simple one. I was not going to entertain the possibility of failure so I concluded that I was a two-talent president. And I've been comfortable with that decision and designation ever since.

Make no mistake—talent is not to be considered as the replacement for hard work. The two go together, not one or the other. I know the value of hard work, as it has been a part of my world all my life. My father taught me the importance of working hard as I saw it modeled in his life from my earliest memories.

[1] Caliguire, Jeff, *The Convergence: Seven Resolves To Release What You Were Born to Do* (Boston, MA: Convergence Point Publishing, 2010), 20.

In my view, my dad was bigger than life. He was offered to play semi-professional baseball and as a young child, I remember thinking the man could do no wrong. Of course, that wasn't exactly the way it was. Dad sold insurance. It was the days of John Wayne, and the "three-martini lunch" and the hard-charging world of the 1950s and 1960s. Dad's friends even called him "Duke." All those martinis would eventually catch up with him, and he would pay the ultimate price.

Growing up, I wanted to be an athlete just like my father. Being active in football, baseball, and basketball was important to me, and I felt like I excelled. That all changed when I was eight and a half years old. I had broken glass kicked into my left eye. As a result, I lost all practical vision in that eye. My ball-playing days were over at eight. But that didn't mean I couldn't transition to a solo sport. I chose to become a member of the school's track team. I ran the half-mile and the mile. I had some pretty good times in those high school races, too—2:06 in the half-mile (we used to refer to it as "run and puke") and 4:53 in the mile.

Our family was a large one—I was the oldest of eight children. It made sense that while I was in high school, I should continue to have a part-time job. My parents helped me get my foot in the door at Food Materials, a Chicago-based company that gave me my introduction to the world of flavors. At sixteen years old, I was sweeping floors and extracting vanilla from beans. Exposure to the company's laboratories led me to choose chemistry as my major as I headed off to the University of Illinois at Chicago. I was working the second shift, and my employer was very understanding about giving me time off if I was behind in my classes and needed to study for a test. In addition, the life experience that I acquired on the job made my studies—especially in marketing and management classes—much more meaningful. It was all a very positive blend for me.

I was struggling a bit with my chemistry classes, as well as foreign language. One day in the early 1970s I was in the school's placement office when I took a look at the job listings and noticed that chemistry majors were earning $8,500, while marketing majors started at $11,000! Plus, there was no language requirement for marketing majors. If I stayed with chemistry, I'd have to take another year of French, which was a course in which I struggled. So that's how I made one of my most important life choices—a move into marketing. I assessed which talents I had, and just as importantly, which ones I didn't have.

It wasn't long before I had made the transition at Food Materials from the laboratory, as an applications trainee, to the sales department. I eventually would become their number one salesperson. I took on additional responsibilities as an assistant to the president and ultimately managed the company's sales and marketing activities.

On an even more personal note, there was another contributing factor to my maturing into a two-talent president. When I was twenty-four years old, I suddenly lost my mother to a blood clot that formed and reached her heart. I took over a major portion of the responsibility for my seven younger siblings. One of my goals was to make certain that all of them would be able to attend college. I'm pleased to say that we achieved that goal for each and every child.

That was my life until I knew it was time to start my own company. In 1987 I established FONA, which stood for our original name, Flavors Of North America. Some people would say it was very risky, at the age of thirty-seven, to leave a very lucrative and secure position and take an 80 percent pay cut. In fact, I was suddenly making about the same money I had previously been paying in taxes. I really believed, however, that there was an opportunity for a small, independent, excellent, service-oriented, and highly technical company.

Finding Your Strengths

God used all my previous life experiences to mold me into a two-talent president. Recently, I accessed the Clifton StrengthsFinder® in order to discover what I can realistically claim as strengths in my life. Here are my top five strengths, along with the definition for each strength as provided by the Clifton group:

- Futuristic—people who are especially talented in the Futuristic theme are inspired by the future and what could be. They inspire others with their visions of the future.

- Belief—people who are especially talented in the Belief theme have certain core values that are unchanging. Out of these values emerge a defined purpose for their life.

- Maximize—people who are especially talented in the Maximizer theme focus on strengths as a way to stimulate personal and group excellence. They seek to transform something strong into something superb.

- Activator—people who are especially talented in the Activator theme can make things happen by turning thoughts into action. They are often impatient.

- Connectedness—people who are especially talented in the Connectedness theme have faith in the links between all things.

They believe there are few coincidences and that almost every event has a reason.

Each of us has our own individual skill set. God has given us strengths, gifts, passions. You have a list of top five strengths, as well. They may be completely different than my list, but that's part of what makes God's design so complete and so fascinating. If you have never taken a StrengthsFinder® or a personality profile (such as the Myers-Briggs Type Indicator®—MBTI®, for example), I encourage you to do so. It's vitally important for all of us to understand exactly what it is that we bring to the game of life. Once we discover who we are and define our personal reality, we can begin the process of assessing where we stand in the realm of being five-talent, two-talent, and one-talent people.

After I took the Clifton StrengthsFinder®, I participated in yet another assessment test that would clearly identify my skill set in more detail. Here is an expanded list of some of my talents:

- I am good at *influencing* other people.

- I excel at *strategizing*, corporately, culturally, and socially.

- I do well at *visualizing*, and by that I mean what I can visualize, I achieve.

- I am good at *futurizing*, meaning I can spot patterns easier than most others.

- I enjoy *designing*, in that I can put together an effective organizational model.

- I do well at *conceiving* not only my own ideas, but also recognizing other's great ideas and helping them work.

- I can *create culture*, rules and values that govern an organization.

- I thrive on *excellence* and challenge myself and others to this end goal.

Once again, I list these, not to focus on myself, but to give you an idea of what a two-talent person might look like. I have a responsibility before God to invest these talents and to gain a return—to see them increase and develop, to bless others with them. I cannot bury these talents in the ground.

What are your talents? Have you ever taken the time to sit down with a sheet of paper and pen in order to write them down? How about some sort of gift assessment? Can you check with your Human Resources Department to see what they might have available to help you along in your quest for answers? Please check with your church for a spiritual gifts assessment. Or pick up Marcus Buckingham's book *Now Discover Your Strengths*, which includes a link to an online version of the StrengthsFinder® assessment.

For some of you who read these words, the concept of five-talent people, two-talent people and one-talent people is a challenging, and even difficult premise to accept. Beside the obvious distinction made by the Lord Jesus in Matthew 25, consider the words of leadership consultant, Dennis Peacocke:

> The heart of modern paganism is to attempt to make equal what God has made unique. . . . Satan hates the uniqueness God has put into His created beings and has transmitted that hatred into all fallen men and systems. God in His sovereign wisdom has chosen to give greater and lesser engiftments to men, and this is like waving a red cape in front of the sin of pride that snorts within our fallen breasts. Satan, and therefore his fallen world system, is totally hung

up on "equality." God, on the other hand, is hung up on individuality or distinctiveness.[2]

The Lord Jesus was not the only One in the Scriptures to affirm the Principle of the Talents. Consider the words of the Apostle Paul:

> There is one Lord, one faith, one baptism, and one God and Father, who is over all and in all, and living through all.
>
> However, **he has given each one of us a special gift** through the generosity of Christ.
>
> —Ephesians 4:5-7 (NLT, emphasis added)

I am different than you. You are different than me. This is the way God made us. Just because I can do certain things better than you does NOT mean that I am better than you. In the same way, you doing certain things better than me does NOT make you better than me. We're all just wired differently. It's the Principle of the Bags of Gold at work.

---

[2] Peacocke, Dennis, *Doing Business God's Way*. (Santa Rosa, CA: Rebuild Press, 2003); p. 123.

CHAPTER FOUR
USE YOUR TALENTS RESPONSIBLY
OR YOU'LL LOSE THEM

*We are entrusted with God's resources in the form of our talents,
skills, abilities, gifts, resources, etc. We have a responsibility to
use them or lose them.*

We are all given our personal resources to manage—and we
have a responsibility to manage them well. As leaders, we
are also entrusted with employees, customers, and stockholders.
One can play this out even further to the point that we are
entrusted with our stakeholder relationships to banks, insurance
companies, and even the government.

Whether we are aware of it or not, this practice plays out in
business all the time. If someone is working on a project and doesn't
perform, he or she will eventually have those responsibilities given
to someone else. So once we know what our talents and resources
are, we have to use them or lose them.

The Principle Found in Matthew 25

The reason five virgins were considered wise and the other five
were considered foolish is directly related to the application of the
Principle of Responsibility.

> At that time the kingdom of heaven will be like ten virgins
> who took their lamps and went out to meet the bridegroom.
> Five of them were foolish and five were wise. The foolish ones
> took their lamps but did not take any oil with them. The wise

ones, however, took oil in jars along with their lamps.

—Matthew 25:1-4 (NIV)

Five of them brought oil with their lamps, five did not. Five were willing to step up to the plate and take responsibility for the talents and/or resources and opportunity they had been given, while the other five missed the opportunity to demonstrate their responsibility. The bridegroom didn't just say, "Oh, it's okay. Come on in anyway." They lost the opportunity to be a part of the wedding because they didn't steward their resources responsibly.

In the same manner, the servants who were given the five bags of gold and the two bags of gold demonstrated that they were willing to use the resources their master had given them. They engaged in the best practice of responsibility.

Again, it will be like a man going on a journey, who called his servants and entrusted his wealth to them. To one he gave five bags of gold, to another two bags, and to another one bag, each according to his ability. Then he went on his journey.

—Matthew 25:14-15 (NIV)

The master "entrusted" his wealth to them, each according to his ability. The master passed along the "bags of gold" (some translations say "talents") to his servants, not just giving them money, but giving them the responsibility to do something with it. This lesson is an important one. The earlier in life we learn to take responsibility for what is ours, the wiser we will be. I will always be grateful that I learned this principle at a young age.

A Test Flight for Responsibility

As a child, I was madly in love with balsa wood model airplanes.

(And it had nothing to do with sniffing the glue!) One of those balsa wood airplane kits would make me about as happy and engaged and contented as you could possibly imagine. There was a fair amount of work involved in putting one together, but through it I learned about the importance of responsibility, of using my talents. If I stepped up to the responsibility to make one, the sweat equity really paid off.

The summer I was eleven years old, I bought a model airplane kit just as the school year was ending. I spent the entire summer working on it. It was a long and sometimes tedious process. I oh so carefully wrapped the wing frames with the tissue paper, and then went through the process of painting on a substance known as "dope," a clear, sticky liquid with the consistency of thick paint or glue. Once the clear dope was dry I put a few more things together and ultimately I painted the entire model with colored paint.

For this particular plane, the Junior Falcon, I remember choosing navy blue with orange wing tips. Finally, I attached the .049 engine to it and she was ready to fly her maiden voyage. I took my responsibility seriously. There was no cutting corners, for this process was truly an act of love. I was fully engaged.

As a boy, I was never quite as close to my father as I had wished to be, but I knew he loved me. He also loved airplanes and flying. He had been in the Army Air Corps as a young man, so I truly hoped that our mutual interest in flying would create a common bond. So I was nervous, pleased, and excited when my dad said he would drive me out to a place where we could try out my newly-finished, navy blue and orange model airplane.

On a crisp, sunny late afternoon in Chicago, I lovingly placed my beautiful airplane on the back seat of the car and gingerly hopped up front on the passenger side to accompany my father to the predetermined location for the flight. Appropriately enough, there was a large field known as the Cumberland Forest Preserve right next to O'Hare Airport, so my small airplane would be able to aspire to fly below the landing pattern of its bigger brothers. Summer had concluded and autumn was in the air, meaning it was a windy, clear day in Chicago. I know that is hard to imagine—wind in Chicago—but just go with me on this one.

When it came time for flying, usually a model airplane of this type was guided by a person on the ground running a remote control unit. But when you're doing things on a tight budget—consisting of money I was making off my paper route—you must get creative. I was still saving my money, so I chose not to purchase a remote control unit. I simply set the controls manually prior to the flight and let the plane do its own work.

Taking full responsibility for its flight plan, I preset the controls for a gentle left bank, meaning the plane would make a circular climbing motion with power or make a descending motion without power. I also pre-arranged for the proper amount of fuel for this voyage. I meticulously measured out enough fuel for a thirty-second test flight. My expectation was that the plane would ascend, make lazy circles in the air, and then descend softly to the ground. I was so excited! What could possibly go wrong?

I fired up the plane's engine and stood back to watch all my hard work pay off. And I must say, in the first few seconds of the flight I experienced exhilaration unlike I had ever felt previously. Truly, the joy of a job well done is one of the benefits (or returns) of using your talents responsibly.

But trouble was brewing, and brewing quickly. I began to notice that instead of a more gradual ascent, as I anticipated, the plane climbed extraordinarily well—much faster and higher than I had expected, too. It went high enough that it became caught up in the unrestricted winds above the forest preserve's canopy of trees. Now I was really flying with the Big Boys, but it was not at all what I had intended. It didn't take long for me to realize where my plane was going and it was not safely back to the ground. It was still climbing.

My model airplane climbed and climbed and then quickly flew away downwind.

Dad and I did our best to chase it down, but to no avail. Not only did it not follow the gentle ascent, lazy circles and smooth descent I had imagined, but it also turned out to have more fuel than the thirty seconds for which I had planned. Thirty seconds actually turned into about ninety seconds and an expeditious climb rate. Dad and I searched and searched for the plane in the adjacent areas of the forest preserve where we thought it might be found. But it was not to be.

Needless to say, it was a long, grieving, and quiet ride home that evening. *No one knows how sad and alone I feel right now,* I remember thinking to myself. *I put so much time and effort into that project and now it's probably resting atop the canopy of trees, gone from my reach and sight forever.* How humiliating for me, especially in front of Dad.

Dad, unaccustomed to offering consolation, drove home without saying a word to me. *Certainly,* I thought, *he could have offered some words of kindness or care or instruction. He could've shared in the responsibility, right?* But the silence was deafening. As I look back on the circumstance, it was probably the first time I realized his inability to create a compassionate connection with me. He loved me, but like the dads of his time, it was love accompanied by distance. There was sadness on many levels that day.

But it certainly provided a lesson in responsibility. I had no one to blame for the loss of that model plane but myself. In the same way, had it followed the flight plan that I had intended, I could have enjoyed the positive outcome of the responsibility as well. I learned it was my responsibility to make good results happen. It would be an important lesson for my future as a business leader. I had learned that it is my job as a leader, even my obligation, to take responsibility of the direction of my company, to plan carefully, make good choices, and lead it accordingly.

Responsibility Is a Leader's Obligation

It is the leader's obligation to use his talents responsibly, or the whole company will pay the price. As the CEO of FONA, I'm acutely aware of my responsibility to all our employees.

Part of the way I embrace that responsibility is to get clear on what it is I need to provide in the way of leadership. What is my role?

Even if you are not a CEO or in management, all of us must be clear on our responsibilities. We are obligated to take whatever talent or position we've been given and responsibly steward it. Whether you're an employee or a business owner, you still must be responsible with what God has given you.

Over the last ten or fifteen years, one of the best illustrations from *The Harvard Business Review* I have seen regarding a leader's obligation to take responsibility is the story of the Proctor and Gamble Company (P&G). A.G. Lafley is the CEO of Proctor and Gamble, a position he assumed in June of 2000. The timing could not have been worse for him. The month he was hired, P&G announced that it would not meet its projected third-quarter earnings, causing the stock to dive from $86 to $60 in one day. The price dropped another eleven percent in his first week at the helm. P&G was truly a company in crisis.

Lafley reflected back on that time during a 2009 article he wrote for the *Harvard Business Review*. He astutely observed:

> ... our biggest problem in the summer of 2000 was not the loss of $85 billion in market capitalization. It was a crisis of **confidence** (emphasis added). Many of P&G's leaders had retreated to their bunkers. Business units were blaming headquarters for poor results, and headquarters was blaming the units. Investors and financial analysts were surprised and angry. Employees were calling for heads to roll. Retirees, whose profit-sharing nest eggs had been cut in half, were even angrier. ...
>
> Everyone was looking to me for answers. ... Welcome to the job of CEO—a job I'd never done before.[3]

Four years later Mr. Lafley sat down with a group of fellow CEO at the feet of the legendary guru of modern management, Peter Drucker. One of the many questions they discussed was: "What is the work of the CEO?"

One of the more profound comments to come out of that discussion was Drucker's belief that the CEO is the link between the "inside," that is, the organization, and the "outside," which is society, economy, technology, markets, and customers. He added that "inside" there are only costs, and results are only on the "outside."

[3] A. G. Lafley, "What Only the CEO Can Do," *Harvard Business Review,* May 2009, 2.

What was Lafley's conclusion to these discussions, added to a decade of experience now under his belt? He told his fellow business leaders:

> . . . if linking the outside to the inside is the role of the CEO, what is the actual work? I think it comes down to four foundational tasks, drawn from Drucker's observations:
>
> 1. Defining and interpreting the meaningful outside.
>
> 2. Answering, time and again, the two-part question: What business are we in and what business are we not in?
>
> 3. Balancing sufficient yield in the present with necessary investment in the future.
>
> 4. Shaping the values and standards of the organization.
>
> The simplicity and clarity of these tasks is their strength, but their simplicity is also deceptive, because the work is more demanding than an observer might suspect. The challenge is to resist getting pulled into other work that is not the unique **responsibility** (emphasis added) of the CEO.[4]

I find it noteworthy that the findings of the Drucker conclave focused around the Principle of Responsibility. Success or failure, progress or digress, all fall on the shoulders of the CEO. The buck stops with that title. Lafley states it this way:

> The CEO is uniquely positioned to ensure that a company's purpose, values, and standards are relevant for the present and future and for the businesses the company is in. The CEO can and must make the interventions necessary to keep purpose and values focused on the outside. To sustain competitive

---

[4] Ibid., 3.

advantage and growth, he or she must create standards to ensure that the company wins with those who matter most and against its very best competitors. . . .

. . . the CEO's real and unique work draws on a uniquely external perspective that is inaccessible to the rest of the organization unless the CEO makes it accessible through choices and actions every day.[5]

Reread that last phrase: "unless the CEO makes it accessible through choices and actions every day." That's the responsibility of the CEO. And all people within an organization have their own responsibility, which they need to clearly understand and embrace.

Responsibility is an obligation. We are each to use our talents not just randomly or foolishly, but responsibly.

The Apostle Paul said it well when he wrote his letter to the church at Galatia: "For we are each responsible for our own conduct" (Galatians 6:5, NLT).

Step up to the plate, my friend. You're up. It's your responsibility.

Have you taken time and effort to grasp what *your* responsibility is? How are you going to fulfill it?

---

[5] Ibid., 8.

CHAPTER FIVE
BE READY FOR THE ACCOUNTING

*There is always an accounting—daily, weekly, monthly, annually. And eventually, there will be a final accounting from God—an external audit of your life and what you did with your talents. There is **always** an accounting.*

Anyone in business is familiar with the idea of accounting—keeping track of earnings and expenditures, determining if a venture is profitable, seeing if a project is completed as it should be. Every successful business makes a habit of regular accounting of its work. Just working hard on something is not enough—we need to see results. When we are working, no matter what task we undertake, we need to keep the end in mind—and be ready for the accounting.

Now, most companies do internal accounting, which is important, but numbers can be manipulated, corners can be cut. However, when there is an audit—an external accounting by a third party—that takes accounting to a new level. And that's the level at which God will ultimately do his accounting of your life.

The strongest text to underscore this Principle is found in the Parable of the Bags of Gold. In verse 19 of Matthew 25 it clearly states: "After a long time the master of those servants returned and settled accounts with them" (NIV).

We also see this practice alluded to in the Parable of the Ten Virgins. At the conclusion of the parable, Jesus exhorts those listening to His teaching: "Therefore keep watch, because you do not know the day or the hour" (Matthew 25:13, NIV).

There will be an accounting, a final accounting, when our lives have ended. Like all final accountings, it's the Biggie. We want to do all we can to be effective with the gifts and talents God has given us. We don't want to miss our opportunity by coming into our task unprepared. Thus, we should be ready at any time for an accounting of our lives and our work, be it daily, weekly, monthly, quarterly, annually, or finally.

If we don't take accounting and accountability seriously, the results can be both embarrassing and devastating. An example comes to mind, based on an association with which I have contact.

Who Is Minding the Store?

I love to fly. I have had my private pilot's license for many years and thoroughly enjoy the experience every time I am in the air. Through my love of flying, I have joined a number of associations that promote flying and aeronautics.

Several years ago, one of these organizations (which shall remain nameless) sent out a letter to members, including me. Apparently, the association had failed to file tax returns for four years, in part because the chief financial officer had not provided sufficient financial data to the executive director.

Payroll withholding, social security, Medicare, and state taxes had all been left unpaid for years, and worse, those unpaid bills were not listed on the organization's financial statements as liabilities.

Apparently, the financial officer decided, because of a lack of cash on hand, simply not to pay the taxes. And then, he didn't tell anyone. The organization put him on leave as they straightened out the mess, which they estimated would cost them as much as $600,000.

A letter from the Chairman of the Board concluded, "This obviously signals a potentially catastrophic situation . . . the single most serious challenge the Society has faced in its 75 year history."

Even with a strategy of accountability and reporting in place at every level of the organization, the CFO figured out a way to engage in some "creative bookkeeping" without anyone else finding out. Without accountability, there is disaster. But there is always an accounting, eventually. Nothing will remain hidden.

My Spiritual Accounting

Some day, there will be a final accounting for all of us. One of the best days of my life was the day I realized that I would ultimately stand before God in order to give an accounting for my very soul. That is one heavy-duty concept, I know, but it is something each and every one of us must face. God had been preparing me my entire life for a decision I would make when I was thirty-three years old. Let me tell you about my spiritual development.

I grew up in a large Roman Catholic family. Some of my earliest memories revolve around the many activities surrounding our local Catholic church. For example, every month we had a service known as the First Friday Mass. I can still remember the priest teaching us that if we went to nine of those First Friday Masses, a priest would be with you when you were at the end of your life in order to administer the Last Rites. I found that to be very comforting and strangely motivational. The Mass was held at 6:45 in the morning, and we were required to fast before it, so we would be in the proper state to take Holy Communion. So, we'd carefully fast, then attend the Mass, but then go straight from Mass to the Catholic school, where our mothers had packed us a breakfast, since we were starving. Because it was Friday, we were not allowed to eat meat, so the food of choice was a hard-boiled egg. It might not sound like much of a delicacy to you, but to a little boy, it was a special treat, eating breakfast at school.

I have very warm family memories from my Roman Catholic heritage. Now, as an adult, I have observed that those who embrace Catholicism do get to know God the Father well. I have also observed that evangelical Christianity helps us get to know God the Son, Jesus better. And the charismatic Christians help us get to know God the Holy Spirit. I intend no type-casting here. Just an obligation for us to know each member of the Trinity as God.

I continued in my Catholic tradition through my growing up years. During my life as a teenager, I attended a youth group that discussed important spiritual issues that I found quite fascinating. There were some healthy debates in which I participated and I remember feeling good about my insight into spiritual issues. But alas, I couldn't give an accounting of my life in any way that would provide a degree of comfort or security. I was just sailing along, spiritually adrift without a rudder or an anchor.

After high school, I attended UIC, the University of Illinois at Chicago, where I felt I had a fairly typical experience as it relates to my spiritual life. Most universities at that time inadvertently, but possibly purposefully, helped you to become an atheist quite rapidly. The compartmentalization of business and science from biblical values had become entrenched. The biology classes centered on evolution. Even classes such as psychology and sociology suggested man was evolving into something better.

Things began changing for me. For example, I had never missed Sunday church until I was in college. During college and during my life, the most shameful personal moral failure I experienced at that time was my poorly thought out but full support of abortion rights. Did I campaign for abortion? No, but just the fact that I embraced it in my mind can still haunt me. But it was a crazy time. It was the end of the conflict in Vietnam; students would be smoking a joint while sitting in class, or protesting something outside of it. In my view it was the closest the United States had come to complete anarchy. We were in a no-win situation.

In my twenties I was experiencing a life that was exactly how I had been raised. As an example, I was regularly using alcohol. Looking back now, I see a family generational abuse of alcohol that I was not aware of at the time. Once out of college, as a young salesman, it was expected and quite common to take customers to the nicest bars and spend money freely on whatever they chose to eat and drink. And naturally, it was only polite to drink along with them. I was sipping Dom Perignon champagne while dining at the finest restaurants, having been driven there with customers in a stretch limousine.

While in college I met a beautiful young woman who completely captured my heart. Her name was Mary and we grew in our relationship by spending a significant amount of time together. We were married in 1979. We are still married today, and she is one of the greatest blessings in my life.

In 1981, we had our first child, Luke. On the outside we seemed like the typical family, happy and carefree. But I still couldn't give an account of my life in any sort of manner that brought lasting peace.

All of that changed in 1983. We weren't really looking for a big change, but it was right on the horizon. Mary and I were invited by some good friends to attend a business conference out west in

Portland, Oregon, and we agreed to spend that time with them. Frankly, I don't remember much of anything from the business portion of the meeting. But what I do remember was that the weekend was life-changing. The group running the conference offered a non-denominational church service the Sunday we were there, so the four of us decided to attend.

As the speaker began to teach, I knew that we were hearing was a different Gospel than anything I had heard before. Mary and I were both very proud of our Catholic heritage, but this presenter was explaining that we could never do enough good works to earn a place with God. No, the only way to make peace with God was to accept what the Lord Jesus did for us on the cross. He died to pay for all our wrongdoings and invites us to receive him as the One who saves us. In accepting Christ as personal Savior, we were guaranteed eternal life because it wasn't dependent on my deeds but on the deed Christ accomplished on the cross.

Both Mary and I were quite moved by this person's simple presentation of the Gospel. I needed a Savior and his name was Jesus. At the conclusion of the message, the speaker gave everyone in the room an opportunity to stand up and come to the front of the room to receive Jesus as Savior. Without hesitation, Mary and I slipped out of our seats and went forward. I later learned that this was a good old-fashioned altar call. We willingly complied. God firmly came and snatched us up, even though we weren't necessarily looking for him at the time.

Things have never been the same since that day. The Lord has been affirming my faith for all these years and continues to do so. When we returned home to the Chicago area, our neighbors Doug and Jane Gault invited us to begin attending church with them at the Hawthorne Hills Community Church (HHCC). We accepted their invitation and immediately started gobbling up the strong teaching from the Bible.

Initially, we straddled the fence by attending a 5:30 Mass at the Catholic church on Saturday evening and then the 9:30 service at HHCC on Sunday morning. Slowly, our involvement with our Catholic tradition faded out of our lives as our biblical foundation grew. This new church experience was centered on Jesus and the teaching of his Word. We were eating it up like a couple of starving peasants at the King's table. Eventually, we ended up at Christ Community Church in St. Charles, near our home. We actively support the ministry there and love how we learn the teachings of the Word.

Why do I share this part of my life with you? Because through my decision to accept Christ as Savior, I have answered the ultimate question regarding the accounting of life. I know I will one day stand before God in order to give account for my life. I can say, with full assurance, that I belong to Jesus, so that God will not see me in all my sin, but rather will see Christ in all his glory. The Apostle Paul put it this way: "For God made Christ, who never sinned, to be the offering for our sin, so that we could be made right with God through Christ" (2 Corinthians 5:21, NLT).

Friend, that's the answer for the final accounting. Are you ready for that appointment? Do yourself a big favor by making that decision right now. This may be your personal altar call. You'll be glad you did. Eternally glad.

CHAPTER SIX
INVEST YOUR TALENTS FAITHFULLY
FOR MAXIMUM RETURN

We will all get the same reward from our master if we use our respective talents properly. He will say, "Well done, good and faithful servant."

Our goal, once we accurately assess our talents and resources, should be to invest them as best we can. As long as we faithfully invest our talents, God will tell us "well done."

As leaders, we not only have to invest our own talents, but we also have to reward the people who work for us when they invest their talents. A business leader can learn something from both the servants and the master in Jesus' parable. We need to give our people a "well done"—but only when it is deserved.

Each of the good servants in the parable of the talents doubled his master's investment. That's a 100 percent return! And he rewarded each of them. While that may seem like a lofty goal, it is possible. In fact, it's what we do regularly at FONA.

The 2 x 4 Principle

As I reflected on the parable of the talents, one business truth clearly stood out to me: we are asked to be faithful stewards and to **double** what has been given to us. I have long noticed that some of the leaders I've observed often had that abundance of success not only in their finances, but in their relationships as well. I've always wanted to understand the reasons.

Perhaps this is why I was so enthralled by Jesus' teaching in Matthew 25. God challenged me in the area of stewardship, but he also clearly spelled out my responsibility to double what he's given me, and helped me to understand the reward for doubling, the penalty for failing, and the accountability in all of the cases.

From a business perspective and as a leader, I came to understand that our responsibility at our company is to double our revenue and results every four years, hence the concept *2 x 4*. It follows the concept that everyone in the company has a responsibility to double their personal results every four years at their level of talent and ability. Doubling is something all people can get their minds around. In contrast, if I announced to our company that I wanted a 19.9 percent compound growth rate for the next four years, that's a bit foreign to the average person. But doubling every four years is the exact same concept as a 19.9 percent growth rate, stated more believably and realistically. So for us it is *2 x 4* or double every four years.

I also think of "doubling" as the "imagination cap." By that I mean that it is the biggest idea that people can both imagine and believe. At FONA, to reinforce this concept, every employee is given a block of wood, a *2 x 4* with a brass plate attached to it. The plate is inscribed with their name and the date they started working at the company. We use it as an object lesson, a reminder of what we expect from them in their daily work assignments. We have found that small block of wood has become a powerful symbol that has taken on even greater meaning over the years.

As for me on a CEO level and on a personal level, I have the obligation—the responsibility—to double business results every four years and double the quality of relationships with key people in my life. It is my intention in this book and in life to practice and to teach Kingdom Economics—our responsibility with the *2 x 4 Principle.*

Investing for Maximum Return Is Its Own Reward

My boyhood paper route taught many valuable business principles. As I said in Chapter Two, it taught me about planning and preparation. And that reward was enjoyed immediately upon receipt of my first monthly paycheck.

I also learned that doing your job well could be followed by a *reward.*

It was a warm day and I jumped on my bike in order to ride down to Rosen's Drug Store. Rosen's was one of those old-fashioned drug stores that today, you can only see in old movies. What made that corner store so special to me was its soda fountain. The counter was an enormous slab of white and black marble, long and narrow, always cool to the touch, with bar stools made of shiny silver metal with soft red pads on top. The stools were on one side and all manner of ice cream treats were on the other.

"I'd like a strawberry malt, please," I asked as I hopped up on the padded stool. I leaned over the counter with anxious anticipation as I watched the server create my reward. As the blender whirred loudly, I could feel my mouth already watering in preparation for what I was about to receive. *Hey, I earned it!* So I can assure you, a strawberry malt never tasted as good as that one did that day. Why? Because I didn't need any of my parents' money to pay for it—I bought it myself with my own money! As I sucked on the straw, the thick malt fighting me every step of the way, I thought to myself, *This is the greatest feeling in the world! What freedom! I don't have to ask my parents for the money to buy stuff, I can do it myself!* I probably didn't even know the word at the time, but I was relishing my newfound state of autonomy. I had just been paid $13.38 for my first month's work. That strawberry malt was worth every penny of the thirty-five cents I was charged.

The other reward of that paper route was autonomy—something that I realized even then was important to me. It wasn't just drinking the malt, but the fact that I didn't have to ask my parents for the money, and could make my spending decision autonomously, that made it so sweet.

A Non-elitist Meritocracy

Today, as a CEO, I continue to invest my talents for maximum return—including the return of satisfaction of a job well done. As I try to motivate my employees to do the same, it's important that the return on their investment include a reward of some kind—like my having my own money and that strawberry malt it could buy.

To engage in the best practice of investing talents for a maximum return, that return has to be something that employees can share in.

One of the values we've established at FONA is "to establish and nurture a high performance work environment." What does that look like?

We compete in an extremely dynamic industry against powerful, resilient competitors. Our primary competitive advantage is our people—our drive, passion, intelligence, and talent.

We recruit, select, and equip best-in-class talent in order to win. One way to find great people and to get them to invest their talents in your organization, is to offer them compelling rewards. They need to know that their investment will bring them a reward beyond just the satisfaction of contributing to a winning team. We provide generous rewards to key financial contributors.

I like to describe our culture at FONA as a non-elitist meritocracy, where the best ideas from dedicated contributors are recognized and rewarded. We expect a great deal from every FONA team member as we continually pursue excellence in our high-performance work environment. We believe that succession management is critical to sustain our organizational performance.

The underlying value in this practice is that of stewardship. We're to invest for the maximum return. In my own business, I have found the best way to communicate this is to remind people of this reality: our job is to steward effectively all of our resources (including our people).

Optimizing our organization requires a disciplined, balanced emphasis on strategy, financial performance and personal accountability.

Stewardship is also closely connected with the principle of excellence. You can't be a good steward and accept mediocrity. At FONA, excellence is imbedded in all of our activities, from technology and innovation through flavor delivery and logistics. We create strategic commitments in our business units where well-researched strategies and plans are developed and executed.

We steward our resources—people, finances, facility—incredibly well—and I'm always casting a vision for improvement. We opportunistically seize business opportunities that others neglect. We believe empowerment and alignment releases potential in people and organizations.

The stewardship of people on your team begins with getting to know them, their strengths and skills, so that you can put them in the right position to optimize their output (and by the way, doing that usually optimizes their job satisfaction, which optimizes their productivity). Giving careful thought to this pays off in many ways.

If we steward our resources carefully and seize opportunities, we'll achieve another of our stated values, which is to outperform our industry in pursuit of profitable growth. If you think about it, growth is simply the "applause" of customers for delivering excellence on every project and opportunity.

A key way to do that, and something that has worked well at FONA, is to make sure every individual is empowered to make contributions to the fiscal health of our organization.

The Principle Found in Matthew 25

The main mention of rewards in this chapter is found in the parable of the bags of gold. Both the servant who was given five bags of gold (or talents) and the servant who was given two bags of gold were rewarded by their master. And they were both praised with the identical words of affirmation and reward: "Well done, good and faithful servant! You have been faithful with a few things; I will put you in charge of many things. Come and share your master's happiness!" (Matthew 25:21 and 23, NIV).

I find it so fascinating that the two servants were rewarded equally with the same words, even though they were given two totally different amounts of money to work with. One would think the master would have given, for lack of a better term, a five-bag-of-gold reward to the servant given the five bags of gold and a two-bag-of-gold reward for the servant given the two bags of gold. And that would have meant that the five-bag-of-gold award was 250 percent better than the two-bag-of-gold award, right? But instead we see that rewards are for all people, at any level and the rewards are given equally. Everyone who invests his talents for the maximum return those talents are able to yield will be rewarded.

"Well Done"

If you were to take an informal survey of the employees here at FONA, specifically to ask them about my style of rewarding, I know one thing that you will hear from just about everyone to whom you speak: I use the words "Well done" only when something exceptional has been accomplished. I reserve those words for outstanding performance.

It's not about perfection because that will never happen. It's not about failure—that would be pure foolishness. It's not about mediocrity because that wouldn't motivate a person to pursue a better way. But it is the response I give when something has been done with *excellence*. (I'll discuss in greater detail those four areas: failure, mediocrity, excellence, and perfection in the next chapter.)

But I want to make clear that I wholeheartedly believe in recognizing and rewarding those who invest their talents in our company. Their faithful investment should not just benefit the company's bottom line. They should receive a personal return as well. As a CEO, I make sure that I (and all of my management team) look for opportunities to affirm and reward our people for their hard work and sacrifice to the company. Recently, we pulled out all the stops and rented a local theater, The Arcada, for an event built around rewarding our employees. If there was any doubt what this event was going to be about, it was clarified the moment one could see the theater's marquee overhanging the front entrance. In big, black, bold letters our people could read:

THE 2010 FONA ACADEMY AWARDS

Loosely based on the Academy Awards ceremony, we put together an evening filled with fun, laughter, warm reflections, and specific rewards given to people who made a difference at our company over the last year. Everyone had a wonderful time. We'll be doing it again, I'm certain.

Over the years I have made a few observations of what works and what doesn't work when it comes to the topic of rewards and return on investment. Let me share a few of my findings.

Never Reward before the Accounting

It seems as if all of us need to learn this lesson on a personal level at least once in our lives before it truly sinks in. Yet, the truth is there—rewarding before the accounting will not conclude with the result which you're expecting.

I saw this concept played out recently by one of our mid-level managers and one of his employees. The employee came to him with a tragic tale of woe. Something had happened at home that required immediate financial attention and our employee was beside himself in sadness laced with panic.

"What am I going to do?" he lamented to his boss.

"Don't worry," our middle manager comforted. "We are a family here at FONA. We will figure out something so that we can be of help to you."

Let me be clear here. Anyone who knows FONA knows that what that manager said to his employee is absolutely true. We just do not leave our people hung out to dry. We *will* do what we can to help them through their crises, in order to eliminate as much of the stress as possible. We've demonstrated that over and over again in our company's history.

It's *how* the manager came up with his solution that led to frustration.

"You know, you are up for your annual performance review in another month," the manager began the conversation the next day with his employee.

"That's correct," he replied.

"Well, I've been thinking," the manager continued. "I know that you are in the middle of a *huge* project for one of our customers that is requiring a lot of extra hours and late nights. We don't have any wiggle room in this project. We *have* to hit the mark within the numbers we've been given."

"Yes, it's been a real struggle to make those numbers work," the employee answered. "But I am confident we can do it."

"That's what I was hoping to hear," the manager said. "In view of that attitude, I am going to assume that you'll nail that project and as a result of that success, I am authorizing a cash bonus that will go toward covering the financial shortfall you are feeling at home. Sound good?"

The employee was thrilled. There were handshakes, hugs, even tears. It was a wonderful moment.

But we need to fast-forward only one month to observe a problem that developed.

Even though the employee had assured his boss that he would make this project happen within the parameters of the numbers, he didn't. Blame it on the stress at home. Blame it on unrealistic expectations. Blame it on wishful thinking. Blame it on whatever you'd like. The truth is the employee was rewarded before the accounting, and it didn't work out the way either manager or employee thought it would.

Hindsight is always 20-20, but this situation was an easy one to predict. The manager should have arranged for financial assistance in the form of a loan for his employee, but he should not have tied it to the project's outcome as a reward. Certainly there were other avenues to explore in order to arrive at the same result financially.

Never reward before the accounting, even if it's based on the best of motives with the hardest-working employees. In order to get a return, you have to invest your talents first.

Rewards Are Not "Fixes"

One of the main purposes of rewards is to let someone know they have done a good job—to provide for them a return on the investment of their time and talents. It is important, therefore, to clarify that rewards are not to be used in an attempt to alleviate some sort of problem situation. For instance, perhaps you have been in the presence of a situation at work where a manager has mistakenly attempted to solve an interpersonal problem between two employees by raising their wages and elevating their positions in an effort to help them "get along better." The two issues simply don't interrelate.

Plus, according to the research quoted by Dan Pink in his presentation, "The Surprising Truth about What Motivates Us," it is not money that is the ultimate motivator in the workplace. It's the knowledge that my work has *purpose*. In many respects, that is the reward in and of itself.

The Ultimate Reward on Earth

Recently, during an interview, someone asked me, "Joe, can you describe your own version of *The Perfect Day* at this point in your life? What would it look like if you could do whatever you wanted to do with whomever you wanted?"

I thought for a moment, but I knew my answer from the instant I was asked. As you'll learn in the next chapter, I'm not into perfectionism. But the best day for me would be a day on vacation with all of our family members.

To make this an official vacation day, it would have to take place somewhere other than our home. It's just too easy to slip back into the pattern of doing work when I know where I can find it at my house. We have a venue—a lodge up in Wisconsin—where we have stayed every year for many years now. The family memories that surround that location are warm, tender, fun, and funny. So get me away from home in order get me into that family memory groove. Once we get that requirement in motion, it really doesn't matter all that much to me what we are doing, because we are doing it together and that's what is important. I am blessed beyond my wildest imagination with the family the Lord has given me. They are a reward far more valuable than any other I possess.

I know that one day I will leave this earthly body and move to my eternal home in heaven. And I also know that there will be a judgment of all I have done here on earth that will result in eternal rewards. But while I am here on earth I think the most wonderful reward is to spend time with the people I love the most.

Most specifically that's my family, but it also includes other members of my "household" as the scriptures call it. My "household" is not only my family, but also those close to me in my employ—like my senior management team. Never mistake the fact that a person can be successful in the business world, while at the same time be a loving family person. It takes work.

It takes planning. But it can be accomplished. I have been more successful with this balance in certain time periods of my life than others—as you might have been as well. I am not holding myself up as the poster boy for perfect balance in all areas of life, but I am of the belief that it is my family that is the sweetest part of the reward for my work.

We all work together and then we will all receive rewards. As the parable illustrated, the servants received the "well done" from their master no matter what amount of money they were given, as long as they did something with it.

Throughout the Bible, we see that faithful investment is rewarded. The Apostle Paul adds his divine insight into this whole subject of rewards: "It's not important who does the planting, or who does the watering. What's important is that God makes the seed grow. The one who plants and the one who waters work together with the same purpose. And **both will be rewarded for their own hard work**" (1 Corinthians 3:7-8, NLT, emphasis added).

CHAPTER SEVEN
AIM FOR EXCELLENCE, NOT PERFECTION

There are only four outcomes at home or at work: failure, mediocrity, excellence, or perfection. Excellence is our target because it requires us and motivates us to get better.

Imagine you are entertaining an important client, or as we call them, partner. Their team visits your facility, where they have a tour and are incredibly impressed. Since we are near Chicago, one option for entertainment when we do this kind of thing is to take a dinner cruise on Lake Michigan, which offers great views of the city skyline. Imagine we take our guests out on Lake Michigan, where we go on an amazing cruise on a well-appointed ship. The lake is flat and calm, the dinner is spectacular, the people all get along and have a great time. The sun sets behind the skyscrapers, and just as the ride ends, we see the fireworks going off at Navy Pier. It is a perfect day. And we think—this is the standard, this is the bar, which all visits from clients should attain.

Believe it or not, that kind of thinking will get us in trouble.

While it is a perfect day, if we try to recreate it, even the next day, we probably wouldn't be able to. Someone might get seasick, the waves might be larger or it could rain. People might not get along perfectly. Perfection—while it's fun when it happens—should not be our standard because it is so difficult to reproduce. When the only acceptable outcome is perfection, we're in trouble.

Most people would agree that excellence is a "best practice" –in fact, the very best practice. But if we don't achieve excellence, what other options are possible? I believe we only have three others: failure, mediocrity, or perfection. I love that kind of simplicity. It reduces the myriad possibilities of a project's outcome to only one of four.

If we can't achieve excellence, what's the next best thing? Many people would select mediocrity. (Although they might not say it out loud, but it's what they do!). They'd put failure at the bottom of the list if they had to say which outcome was preferable.

That's a mistake. The second best option is failure. Let me explain. If I fail at a task, I have, as Thomas Edison said, figured out yet another way not to do what I'm trying to do. Failure is actually only a temporary problem, because I can fix it.

However, if I do an "okay job," that's a problem. Mediocrity is the biggest threat to excellence, since the job is completed, but in a mediocre fashion. I can also attempt to complete the job perfectly, without flaw, which sounds good, but in reality is an unrealistic goal that actually leads to procrastination.

That leaves *excellence*. Doing the job well is the option I want in my every venture. It's essential to get it beyond right. My goal is not just to get it right, nor to get it perfect, but to "get it excellent!" I relentlessly pursue excellence for the joy of excellence and for the hope of hearing, "Well done, good and faithful servant" from God at the beginning of my arrival in Heaven.

The Importance of Excellence

Allow me to offer another personal example. From the time I was a youngster, I have had a love of flying. More than likely, I inherited that love from my father, who also shared in that feeling. In World War II, Dad was attending flight school in the Army Air Corps when the end of the war was announced. I can still recall with great fondness the hours I would spend at home, paging through his Aviation textbook, dreaming of the day when I would be an adult, and I could sit in the pilot's seat in the cockpit and take off in my airplane to any place I wanted to go.

My parents encouraged this love of flying in my life by taking me down to Chicago's Lakeshore Drive every year to see the Air Show. I still get tingles thinking about the Blue Angels, The Thunderbirds, and all manner of precision flight teams that would perform in flawless formation throughout the day. I just loved it. There was an excitement surrounding flying that got a hold of me.

I also can recall when I was around nine or ten years old, my dad put me in the back seat of a Piper Cherokee while a friend of his took us up for a flight around the area. Looking out the window to the earth down below was a thrill, but it was the collection of gauges, knobs, and other equipment in the front of the cockpit inside that had me utterly mesmerized and fascinated. It was an excellent adventure that has stayed with me to this very day.

If it were not for the injury to my left eye that occurred when I was eight, I probably would have pursued a career in aviation, be it commercial or military. Looking back, I believe God spared me from a circumstance that could have been devastating. Based on my age and my love of aviation, had I chosen to fly, I would have most likely ended up as a military pilot, and the odds are that I would have been sent to fly over Vietnam. Visions of John McCain and his stay at the Hanoi Hilton or some other prisoner of war camp flash through my mind, and I thank the Lord for having a different plan for my life.

So I remained in the states, pursuing my business goals in the flavor industry. But while in my twenties, I studied, practiced, and ultimately received my glider license. Years later—about ten years ago, I earned my Private Pilot Power Certificate for single engine aircraft. And that is an accomplishment of which I am very proud. I can still remember the intensity of preparing for the exam. It is a very thorough test, with no room for goofs. Excellence is not just a goal, it's necessary for survival.

Which brings me to my point. The next time you are flying commercially, when you are in the air sitting comfortably back in the passenger cabin, you trust that the pilot is going to do things in an excellent manner. You would think it's a joke being played on you, if early in the flight the pilot announced over the loudspeaker, "Ladies and gentlemen, welcome on board. I'm going to turn the controls over to my copilot, Bob Johnson, and I'm told he is quite mediocre at what he does. Thank you for flying with us." You're not necessarily requiring perfection, but you do want excellence. Mediocrity just won't do.

So, if that is the standard for a commercial pilot, why shouldn't that be the standard for a leader? A sales force? A management team? A flavors company? A mother or a father?

I have learned from my earliest experiences as a CEO that excellence should be part of the job description. If you lead in a mediocre manner, that same or greater mediocrity is the response you will get from your team. The leader always has to go a bit beyond what he expects from his employees. The leader's efforts and values are always duplicated, for better or for worse.

As obvious as a commitment to excellence may sound, it's not as simple an assignment as one may think. Many of us note that we are no longer in a culture that stresses excellence and part of the reason lies in the fact that we live in a culture that views the whole concept of "work" as toil, drudgery, even a curse on them.

Rather than rejoicing in the ability to put our gifts and talents on display, we view excellence as "just too much work to achieve." We don't realize that excellence is in many ways its own reward— it can bring us joy if we pursue it by engaging our unique talents and strengths. Sadly, it is often Christians who are caught in the midst of all this tension.

Business consultant Dennis Peacocke rightly observes: "What will it take for America to learn that taking the Christian influence out of our national public life is a catastrophic economic choice as much as anything else."[6]

Later in the same chapter, he adds:

Let's turn up the heat for **Christian excellence** (emphasis added). For years deterioration in both the quality and the quantity of work has occurred in much of the United States. The solution begins with Christians renouncing and repenting from their anti-work attitudes. . . . We won't see a fundamental change in our economy until the Church repents of its anti-work attitude and views work as a blessed call to which Christians commit themselves just as God does.[7]

Excellence will never happen unless we see our talents as a wonderful gift from God, not as an impossible assignment. We need to believe and embrace the truth that God has gifted us so we can work diligently to create excellence in our craft. And excellence is appropriate in every environment. I do my best when times are good. I do my best when times are bad. Either

[6] Peacocke, Dennis, *Doing Business God's Way* (Santa Rosa, CA: Rebuild Press, 2003), 53.
[7] Ibid., 59.

circumstance is the right one for me to pursue character and a lifestyle wholly immersed in excellence.

The Principle Found in Matthew 25

In the Parable of the Bags of Gold, the servant who was given five bags of gold, or talents, gained five more. And the servant who was given the two bags or gold, or talents, gained two more. Each of these servants doubled what was given to them. If there are only four possible workplace outcomes—failure, mediocrity, excellence, or perfection—it seems clear that these two servants stepped up to the plate and produced a result characterized by excellence.

In the story of the sheep and the goats, those who received the "well done" from Jesus were those who stepped up and made excellent efforts to help others. They didn't solve every problem of hunger or pain in the world, but they made excellent effort. They didn't just accept things the way they were (mediocrity) but rather tried to change them. They, too, aimed for excellence.

Excellence In Times of Trouble

One might suggest that it is much easier to engage in the practice of aiming for excellence when things are going well; however, the truth is that both good things and bad things happen on a daily basis. When a bad thing occurs, our response can be a significant source of excellence. An incident here at FONA a while ago clearly illustrates this concept.

It began like any other typical day at our FONA facility. Perhaps the only circumstance that could be considered out of the ordinary was the replacement of a safety valve that was in need of routine preventative maintenance. Outside, the clouds began to cover the sky with a dark, ominous look. We were in for a thunderstorm.

We were processing a flavor when it happened. We still don't know what caused it, but it shook the entire plant like a bomb had been dropped in the center of the building.

Everyone stopped working, wondering what was going on. It turned out that a pressure cooker seal had failed and tossed off its sizeable, heavy stainless steel lid, releasing the pent-up air pressure, as well as about two hundred pounds of product.

Thankfully, all our people were safe.

But what a mess! We're a food company, so the one thing you cannot have is what is referred to as a "microbiological failure," or what we call a "micro hit." In other words, contamination of any kind is not acceptable. What if the pressure failure led to airborne micro-contamination in our foods? As a routine precaution and to check on the health of our employees, the fire company was called. They began by reporting, incorrectly, on their radios, "There's been an explosion at the FONA factory!" Of course, the word *explosion* was quickly picked up by the local media, and we had a full-scale circus on our hands.

We immediately assessed what had happened and what was going on. It was clear that we had some major clean up to do, but for me, there was also the issue of how I was going to handle this situation in a way that inspired excellence. If it was not done properly, not only would we have a crisis, but we would add to it a crisis of confidence.

Thankfully, no one was seriously injured, but the paramedics took two of our folks to the hospital, one because of ringing in the ears and another just to be looked over in a precautionary manner. (The media also had a good time inflating the seriousness of the hospital visits.)

Remember, we are a highly sanitary company with "clean room" standards for our production facilities. When the fire department arrived and entered the building, they broke that sanitary seal. Sales and marketing were alarmed, wondering out loud how we would keep our orders going and what this would do to the future growth of our company.

Acting according to our contingency plan, we called our insurance company who came out immediately and oversaw the clean up of the entire situation. And when I say our clean up, I mean micro tests on over seven hundred products and on over three hundred environmental swab samples.

It is important to re-emphasize that this was a sudden release of pressure, not a fire. We found ourselves asking questions such as, "How will this affect other departments at FONA? How do we know the "stuff" that released isn't in the HVAC? Is it in our drain system? Is everyone clear on the fact that we will have a much worse problem if we have just one micro failure?"

The reason I refer to this incident at this juncture is because it was the perfect opportunity to lead with excellence. It was not business-as-usual that day. It was quite the contrary. But what a window to display what it looks like to go beyond good to great. Remaining calm, our team formed and handled this situation precisely as we should have and even went the extra mile to insure all was aboveboard. In all honesty, I wouldn't want to go through a similar circumstance again, but it was an important chapter in the story of excellence at FONA.

For the Christian, excellence is just one more way to give testimony to what God has done for us in our individual lives. Plus, it's a way to show folks exactly how the Lord Jesus would handle situations, were he still physically present here on earth.

Excellence is summed up beautifully in the words of the Apostle Paul, in his letter to the church at Colossae: "And whatever you do or say, do it as a representative of the Lord Jesus" (Colossians 3:17, NLT).

CHAPTER EIGHT
BE STRONG AND COURAGEOUS

Fear, though a normal part of life, can cause us to bury our talents. Fear and perfectionism both create procrastination.

Every day, each of us comes to work with a certain level of fear. If we don't, we are seriously under-challenged. Sometimes, we have fears about our work, or worries about our families, or other stresses. Fear is normal, and in some ways, fear is motivating. It makes us realize we have to give our best effort to overcome the challenges before us.

If we let fear rule us, however, it will paralyze us. The best practice when it comes to fear is to acknowledge our fear (boldly telling the truth about it) but then choose to be courageous in the face of it.

Up to this point we've maintained a very positive approach as we've discussed best practices for success. But to be fair, it is important to note that this passage of Scripture also includes some stern warnings about what to avoid in our approaches to business and to life. Implicit and explicit in the Lord's teaching is this firm advisory against being enslaved to fear. I recently heard that the words "Do not fear" or "Do not be anxious" are the number one commandments stated by Jesus. Likewise, the same concept is also frequently repeated in the Old Testament scriptures, either as "Fear not" or in a positive way, "Be strong and courageous." Fear exists. To "fear not" is to choose not to let it run your life. Thus, it is an important concept to master. Unlike the other principles that bring out the best in us, embracing fear will only bring out our worst. But courage is always a best practice.

The Principle Found in Matthew 25

Up to this point we've talked a great deal about the servant who was given five bags of gold (talents) and the servant who was given two bags of gold (talents) . They both serve as exemplary models of several of the principles we've unearthed in our study together. But what about the servant who was given one bag of gold (one talent)? He really didn't do anything with it, did he?

When it came time for him to give an account of what he had done while his master was gone, he uttered the following words:

> "Master," he said, "I knew that you are a hard man, harvesting where you have not sown and gathering where you have not scattered seed. So I was afraid and went out and hid your gold in the ground. See, here is what belongs to you."

> —Matthew 25:24b-25 (NIV, emphasis added)

Fear Causes Paralysis

The behavior of this particular servant is very instructive. Undoubtedly, there are many issues at work here, but we can say for certain that this servant was paralyzed by his fear.

But he wasn't the only one who was afraid, from my view of this account. Although the Matthew 25 text doesn't address it specifically, I would suggest that there was equal fear among all three of the servants. Everyone, every day, shows up fearful about today's work assignments, to some degree. And if we don't work through the fear, in order to overcome it, fear will almost always lead to paralysis.

One of the main ingredients contributing to fear in our lives is the fear of failure. "What if I attempt this new project and I fail miserably?" we say to ourselves. But to paraphrase a brilliant sentiment by Jim Collins, author of *Good To Great*, we shouldn't fear failure as much as we should fear mediocrity. (I refer you back to the previous chapter).

Fear also causes us to procrastinate while waiting for perfect conditions to develop. As I look back on some of my business decisions, I must admit that I most likely put off starting FONA, using that same theory. "Maybe I can start my own business once some additional elements fall into place," I can hear myself saying. Yet, as you overcome those individual fears in your life, you begin to build up energy, confidence, and freedom. And you need all three of those qualities to start a successful business. It was an important moment in my life when I felt the freedom to become an entrepreneur.

Every one of us faces fears in our life. "My phone call will never be returned," the salesperson laments. "The next project won't go as well as this one has gone," admits the middle manager. "Our flavor won't be approved by our customer," a FONA employee silently concludes. "People won't respond favorably to my leadership style," a young and relatively inexperienced leader privately laments. Ironically, these statements only compound our fear because they are not necessarily based on truth. In reality, the phone call will be returned, the project will be well done, the flavor will be approved. But fear can become a self-fulfilling prophesy.

As we already stated, a most common form of fear is the "fear of failure." I can still remember being almost terrified to make a sales call on one of the largest food companies in the world because I was afraid I would fail.

But ironically, I have also observed people who experience "fear of success." "What if I make this sales call and end up coming back with their business? I really don't deserve to have a customer of this stature, so I think I'll just avoid making the call in the first place!" Or, we're afraid that if we get the order, we won't be able to fulfill itso we'll disappoint the customer or our boss. Fear of success happens when you tell yourself: "I am frightened I can't deliver what I've offered, so I think I'll just avoid the call in general, and spare myself the agony." It stems from feelings of inadequacy, of not being good enough.

It is my job as the CEO to help my people overcome their fears. What techniques do I use? I believe the tool that best fights fear is *the pursuit of excellence*. It is that vitamin shot that gives you the confidence to move forward.

Fear leads to paralysis. It keeps me "stuck" where I am, rather than letting me go where I want to be. When someone is procrastinating, it is often because they feel afraid. One practical technique I use that proves to be effective in combatting procrastination (and therefore fear) is helping people develop a firm "stop time" rather than a "start time." This involves getting the person to clearly decide a specific time when they will stop working on a project if they are struggling to get it started or keep it moving. In this way, the person moves on to another project, rather than feeling that frustrating, wheel-spinning experience of getting nowhere fast.

"Stop time" works at home, too. For example, instead of asking my teenage daughter when she will begin her homework, I ask her when she will *stop* doing her homework. "I will be done with my homework by eight o'clock so I can watch *The Bachelor* on TV," she responds with a big grin on her face.

I was asked recently if I face large amounts of fear in my role as CEO at FONA. There isn't much that scares me in my role with the people in our company. I love the interactions I have with them and we all get along quite well. But I'll tell what does strike fear in my life. It may sound a little odd to you, but it's scary to me when I look out my office window to the company parking lot, filled with cars. Focusing on one car at a time, I find myself overcome with a singular thought: *Look at all those car payments!*

It is the sudden and weighty realization that I am responsible for the paychecks that will go toward making all those car payments. And then, by extension, the house and rent payments. That reality can really stir a sobering, but highly motivating, fear in my life.

Fear Inhibits Entrepreneurship

Earlier in my business career, once I moved through many of my fears, I was in a place where I could exercise my entrepreneurial tendencies by starting FONA. As I look back on those days, I now have concluded that the pressure of entrepreneurship either makes you a better person or a worse person. I learned a great deal about myself, and about entrepreneurship, during those days.

First, I learned that entrepreneurship puts pressure on your character. There are constant temptations to take shortcuts, cut corners, and do less than expected. Add to this pressure the fact that employees, customers, and coworkers are constantly watching you, and you begin to realize that your character and reputation are routinely on the line. If you let fear step in, it only gets worse.

Secondly, as a result of the added pressure on my character, I found this was a time in my life to seek the wisdom of others. Fear grows when we think we're all alone. So seeking out others who can offer wisdom and support will banish that fear, enabling you to be strong and courageous as you meet the challenges of your work. I earnestly tracked down good ideas from leaders, both historical and contemporary, in order to bolster my leadership arsenal. Most significantly, I was constantly driven to the Bible, where the honest answers to the ultimate questions could be found, spoken by God himself.

Thirdly, the entrepreneurial spirit made me more prayerful. I regularly beseeched God for his direction on the many decisions I was making on a daily basis. He has never let me down!

Finally, becoming an entrepreneur drew me closer to my wife, Mary. The closeness wasn't anything new to Mary, who had always drawn close to me. But I was now moving toward her, and I found that as a result, I became a better person.

Fear and Missed Opportunities

Think about all the opportunities we miss because we are afraid.

- The calls we never made.
- The contracts we never signed.
- The business relationships we never developed.
- The new companies we never created.

With my love of flying one would think I might have all sorts of personal recollections involving frightening moments in the air. But actually, the opposite is true. I've had mostly smooth flying in my years of flying as a private pilot. There is, however, one remembrance I have involving a bit of fear and stress. But it took place on the ground.

A friend of mine was in the copilot's seat, and I sat to his left in a small plane preparing for takeoff at our local airstrip, the DuPage

Airport in West Chicago. All was well, everything was going as usual. We started down the runway for our takeoff, and we lifted off when suddenly there was a deafening sound that bombarded our plane. Turning our heads towards the noise, we quickly determined that the plane's right door had popped open. We reached over, grabbed the door, and pulled it tightly shut. But in that small window of time during the climb, the noise really was beyond loud.

Unbeknownst to us, the control tower had instructed us to adjust our route to 200 degrees and make a left turn. Neither my friend nor I had the ability to hear the tower due to the noise created by the open door. Missing a message like that could have been disastrous, since the tower gave us those instructions in order to keep us a safe distance from other aircraft. Later we would find out that the tower concluded we didn't hear the message, since we didn't respond, so it gave another plane instructions to "go around" and avoid coming too close to us.

There really wasn't any danger, and with the exception of the fact that the gentleman in the control tower was quite ticked off at us, there was no damage done. But because of the door opening at that inopportune time, we had to divert our focus to the stressful situation at hand and consequently we missed the opportunity to hear and to do what the tower instructed. A millisecond of fear made a big difference. I've heard it said that once a person becomes afraid, one of the first senses to go is the sense of hearing. Certainly, when I see a person in the workplace who is afraid, I already know he isn't listening to me, or the people around him. He's tuning everything out, or listening to the voice of fear in his head. That is very similar to the "one-talent servant."

Fear can cause us to miss opportunities, so we must be diligent to face our fears, work through them, and be successful with the talents and gifts we've been given.

In the Old Testament book of Joshua, we read the story of the Israelites preparing to go into battle to take over the Promised Land. God tells Joshua to be "strong and courageous." He tells him to be confident. Why? Because Joshua is a brilliant war general? Not really. The only reason for Joshua's lack of fear, according to the Bible, is this: "for the LORD your God will be with you wherever you go" (Joshua 1:9, NIV). We can be courageous not because of our own abilities, but because God is with us. He's given us talents and strengths, and he'll walk with us as we use them to succeed.

These words from the Psalms offer similar encouragement of God's presence with us when we face our fears:

> God is our refuge and strength, always ready to help in times of trouble.
>
> So **we will not fear** when earthquakes come and the mountains crumble into the sea.
>
> Be still, and know that I am God!
>
> —Psalm 46: 1–2, 10 (NLT, emphasis added)

Fear is normal. We can choose whether it will motivate us to engage in the practice of being courageous, or we can let it paralyze us. The determining factor in how we see and respond to fear is our awareness of God's presence. So cling to that presence, friend. God cares about your business life and will be with you and give you courage.

Chapter Nine
Redistribute Unused Talents and Resources

Unused gifts, resources, and talents are always recycled to someone who will use them faithfully. When we don't use our gifts, they'll be given to someone else.

In God's economy, nothing is wasted. God recycles. This is something God does, and something we should do as leaders, and we should encourage those we lead to do the same.

God entrusts us with talents, as we've established. But sometimes, we, like the foolish servant, bury our talents, and don't use them. This is a "best practice" that is also an observation of what will naturally happen in life and in business; if we don't make best use of a resource, it will be taken away, redistributed to someone else for investment. If we fail to get a return on our investment, we will be stripped of the privilege and responsibility to steward those gifts.

As a leader, I must be aware of what talents my people possess, and whether or not they are using them to maximize a return. If they are burying talents, I may have to step in and reassign responsibilities—in other words, redistribute resources or assignments. It's vital to the success of our business.

This is also an observation about how life works: in a free market, resources get recycled, and if you don't do well with what you're given, you're going to lose it.

But sometimes, we must decide to redistribute resources ourselves. Sometimes you may find yourself working on something that doesn't fit—or a project that someone else may be much better at. It's better to hand off that assignment to someone better suited to it. You can offer that person the resource of your assistance, or just free them to run with a project so that you can focus on developing your own talents.

This practice is not about God being punitive, but rather, holding his servants accountable. On the other hand, it's also about us being generous. If you have resources you aren't using, give them to someone who can use them. Take the initiative to recycle resources and everyone benefits.

Imagine if I, as CEO, refused to hire employees, because I didn't want to share the resources of my company by paying other people. I tried to do the work of all the people—the flavor chemists, the sales team, the janitors, truck drivers, everyone! That would be a recipe for disaster, not to mention ridiculous. Our company has responsibilities, and we share those with our employees. It also has financial resources, and we share them with our employees. When we spread those responsibilities and rewards with others, we succeed together. We get more done, and do it better than if one person tried to do it all himself.

The Principle Found in Matthew 25

As we continue to look at the three servants who were given bags of gold by their master, we observe that the servant given one bag of gold was afraid and that fear paralyzed him from doing anything with the gold. It is the response of the master that is the next facet of our investigation. What can we learn from the subsequent interaction between these two men that can be applied to our lives today?

In our previous chapter we saw how the servant who had been

given one bag of gold became paralyzed by fear, which resulted in him not doing anything with the bag he had been given. But that is not the end of the story for that particular servant. His master was deeply disappointed with his behavior—he even described it as "wicked" and "lazy." Notice the end of the parable:

> His master replied, "You wicked and lazy servant! So you knew that I harvest where I have not sown and gather where I have not scattered seed? Well, then, you should have put my money on deposit with the bankers, so that when I returned I would have received it back with interest.
>
> "So **take the bag of gold from him and give it to the one who has ten bags**. For whoever has will be given more, and they will have an abundance. Whoever does not have, even what they have will be taken from them. And throw that worthless servant outside, into the darkness, where there will be weeping and gnashing of teeth."

> —Matthew 25:26-30 (NIV, emphasis added)

In today's world we would use the clichéd phrase—use it or lose it!

The more positive aspect of the practice of redistribution is also seen in the story of the sheep and the goats. Jesus commends those who "gave me something to eat" or "clothed me" and so on, saying that what they'd done for "the least of these" they had done for him.

The "least of these," by definition, do not have enough resources. Jesus asks his followers to free up resources they are not using and generously share them with those in need. If we have resources that we are not using, or that we can sacrifice for the good of others, Jesus tells us we will be rewarded if we share those with others. What we hoard, eventually, will be taken from us.

Use It or Lose It

What helps a person get into the mode of regularly using the gifts he or she has been given? Part of the answer lies in the realm of discipline, and another part of it revolves around enjoyment.

At FONA our customer service philosophy is simple . . . retain 100 percent of our business. That translates into a working relationship with each of our customers that is characterized by excellence and the willingness to go the extra mile to make certain that they are satisfied. And of course that requires personal discipline on our part. FONA employees do what they need to do to make satisfaction an every day occurrence. If it requires coming in early and staying late, that's what takes place. We want to take care of our customers so they don't ever feel like they want to go elsewhere. If you want your clients or customers to be happy, it doesn't happen automatically; you must work for it.

It's a lot like cultivating the discipline of getting regular physical exercise. Many years ago the doctors helped me determine that my life as a runner was over. It was just too much for my injured right knee. But we all agreed that I still needed a consistent form of exercise. A viable alternative to running was walking. As a result, I become a walker—a serious walker. How serious?

*I have walked **every single day** over the past seventeen years!*

Honestly. I am not exaggerating. I can tell you exactly when it began. On August 1, 1994, I started a routine of walking a minimum of at least 25 to 45 minutes a day. I am an early riser so when I am not on the road traveling, I like to walk early in the morning. I listen to the Bible on my iPhone® as I walk. (When I first began walking, I would read the Bible, which gave way to listening to cassette tapes on a Sony Walkman®, which led to CDs, then an iPod®, and finally the iPhone®.) If I am traveling or in some sort of early morning business meeting, I may not get to walk in the morning, but I make sure I get a walk in before retiring at night.

I remember thinking during that first week of walking that a person can acquire a new habit by doing something for seven straight days. There's an even greater probability if you can do it for twenty-one successive days. Forty-five days makes an even stronger case, and ninety days is just about a certainty. I passed through those portals and have continued to do it ever since. Ninety days has turned into somewhere around 6,575 days!

Why do I share this story of walking with you? Because, if you want to be a walker, you've got to walk. If you want to be a runner, you've got to run. If you want to keep your customers happy, it's summed up in the Nike slogan—*just do it!*© Sure, it will require discipline, but it's a discipline that is rewarded. If you don't work hard to keep your customers, they will be "redistributed" to your competitor because your competitor is much more willing to take care of them and do what is necessary to keep them happy. Practice discipline to keep this principle from happening to you.

Another aspect of keeping your customers is cultivating the practice of *enjoyment*. In terms of redistribution, if I don't enjoy what I'm doing, it will most likely be taken away from me. When I am not experiencing enjoyment, it's only natural for me to look at how to cut corners, do less than 100 percent, just to get by. As an example, you know that I love to fly. There was plenty of study and hard work required for me to get certified as a private pilot. But it was all worth it to me because I so enjoy the experience of being airborne!

It's the little things that make the difference. Jesus said in Luke 16:10 (NLT): "If you are faithful in little things, you will be faithful in large ones."

If I don't change the oil in my car regularly, ultimately I may lose the whole car. If I don't enjoy pleasing my customers and helping them meet their needs, they will recycle to someone else who will. Learning to enjoy even the small aspects of life, the small things in my relationships, the small things in my everyday world, will all go a long way toward my keeping the strengths I've been given. Use it or lose it!

A Promotion for the Paperboy

Early in the book I regaled you with my earliest job as a paper boy for the *Chicago Daily News*. There were so many lessons I learned through that experience that stay with me to this day. Actually, there is even more to the story than I have already shared. And the addition is a perfect illustration of the practice of redistribution.

I so enjoyed throwing the papers every day, and in doing so with such satisfaction, I must have somehow caught the attention of some of my superiors. Only two years after I began, at the ripe old age of ten, I was approached by my boss with an important question: "Joe, we have another position here at the paper that has become available. We believe you can handle it, along with your regular paper route. How would you like to be my man in charge of collections?"

"What's that mean?" I asked, excitedly. I was interested, but I didn't know what I might be getting into.

"Well," he cleared his throat and began with an even more serious tone in his voice, "many of our customers pay their bill directly by mail for their paper. But there are some who need a visit from someone representing the newspaper agency in order to collect what's due on their unpaid bill."

"So, I go to people's houses and get the money from them?" I concluded with my excitement growing.

"That's correct. The best day to do it is on Saturday, and the best time on Saturday to do it is in the morning. We've had another young man doing it, but he hasn't been all that effective. So . . . are you willing to give it a try?"

"I'm your man!" I responded with typical ten-year-old confidence.

But I wasn't just speaking out of pure childish ignorance. I knew I could make this job one that worked for me, so I was thrilled for the opportunity.

It was one of the first steps in developing my gifts in the whole area of sales and the development of personal relationships. I found that I could be nice and polite and grateful, while at the same time communicating the fact that we needed the cash in order to settle up their account. To the delight of my boss, I had found a real niche in the collections job.

I'll always remember the first Saturday I gave collections a try. Bright and early (but not too early) I was on my bike, moving from address to address, ringing doorbells. I have no idea how I compared with the young man who preceded me, but I know that after one morning of collecting, I was able to present my boss with the grand total of . . . three hundred dollars!

It was an all-time Saturday morning record!

My boss was ecstatic, which makes me think I was a better fit for this position than my predecessor. It was redistribution in motion. The young man who preceded me didn't give the job the care and attention that I did, and as a result, the position was redistributed to me. I was better suited to it, and gave more energy and effort to it, and got better results.

I used the position faithfully and was rewarded accordingly. Once I turned in the money I had collected, my boss explained the payout. "Great job, Joe! You really came through for us and that is terrific. So let me explain how we pay you for what you've done."

I leaned in with optimistic anticipation in order to get the full effect of the explanation that followed.

"We will give you a five percent commission on everything you bring in for us. So, today you turned in three hundred dollars—here's your fifteen-dollar commission!"

Now, don't forget, I was throwing papers five days a week for a little over thirteen dollars a month. So fifteen dollars for a morning's work was like winning the lottery. Redistribution was working in my favor.

And it can work in your favor, too. If you have a job responsibility that you are shirking, now is the time to get busy with your full attention. If you don't, the responsibility may be taken from you and given to someone else. There are others who are reading these words who will be the people that will be tapped to take on new and additional responsibilities as a result of the redistribution. Be prepared and do your very best work.

It's all about being good at what you do and being faithful enough to be trusted with the task.

Paul the Apostle stated it succinctly: "Now, a person who is put in charge as a manager must be faithful" (1 Corinthians 4:2, NLT).

Friend, use it or lose it!

CHAPTER TEN
EXPRESS GRATITUDE TO GOD
AND OTHERS

Gratitude is our first priority and it precedes all rewards.

What you have has been entrusted to you by God—whether you acknowledge that truth or not. And even the most ambitious person has had others help him along the way. No one is entirely "self-made." That's why it's essential to express gratitude to God and others. It will help you to stay appropriately humble, but also, it will further your success because people want to help someone who regularly expresses gratitude.

One of the surest marks of a grateful person is a generous spirit. As it says in the Bible, freely have you received, freely give.

These two attributes are intimately connected. Generosity is the outpouring of a grateful heart. One of the most important of our seven values at FONA is that of sharing generously, not only with our employees but also with the community around us. We regularly give at least a tenth of our post-tax earnings to local charities. We've been recognized for our generosity and volunteerism in the community. We also make sure that we invest in our people to show them our gratitude for their hard work.

The people of FONA display incredible amounts of warmth and regard for each other. We bring individual contributors together into a workplace community where the individual experiences respect and care.

In order to be generous to our employees, we make sure that our benefits are among the richest in the industry, reflecting our belief that if you take good care of your people, they will take good care of your customers and the business.

We strive to balance short-term care of our employees with enabling opportunities for their long-term growth. We recognize that we do not exist for ourselves; FONA makes a vital and necessary contribution to our larger communities and our industry communities. We want to respond to the way our business has succeeded by being grateful and showing that gratitude with generosity.

I am grateful that you have stayed with me through these practices, which are the ingredients for success. I hope you feel rewarded as a result. Gratitude precedes rewards, so as you launch out to apply these principles in your life, know that I am grateful you invested the time in digesting what has been presented. Let's make one final visit to Matthew 25 to see what God's Word says about gratitude.

The Principle Found in Matthew 25

In the Parable of the Bags of Gold, the master was attentive to the fact that he should express gratitude to the man who had received five bags of gold, as well as to the man who had received two bags of gold. He expressed his genuine thanks by using the same words to both servants: "Well done, good and faithful servant! You have been faithful with a few things; I will put you in charge of many things. Come and share your master's happiness!" (Matthew 25:21 and 23, NIV)

We also see gratitude displayed in the teaching concerning the sheep and the goats: "Then the King will say to those on his right, 'Come, you who are blessed by my Father; take your inheritance,

the kingdom prepared for you since the creation of the world' "
(Matthew 25:34 NIV).

The seed thought buried beneath that expression by the King
is a genuine expression of gratitude for the faithful qualities
exemplified by the sheep. That faithfulness expressed itself in the
generosity his sheep showed to others. In turn, the King expressed
his gratitude with generosity toward them.

As I have already mentioned, the people that work for me know
when I'm really serious about recognizing them for excellent
work. I want to keep it simple so I say, "*Well done.*" I take my cue
from the scriptures—"Well done, good and faithful servant." Not
only does God reward those who are faithful in the little things,
but he also expresses his gratitude.

Gratitude for the Little Things

From the time I was young, I learned to be grateful for even the
little things in life. As Americans, we are guilty of overlooking a
great many blessings that we've received both individually and as
a nation. One needs only to travel outside our borders to realize
how truly blessed we are.

I remember as a child being grateful for simple things, like food
to eat, a roof over my head, and a bed to sleep in. Especially a bed
to sleep in. Let me explain.

Growing up in the Chicago area in the fifties and sixties, we were a
large family. For most of the time in our family's early history, there
were eight children, a mom, a dad, and a grandmother all under
one roof. It really wasn't that uncommon back then, but it sounds
rather out of the ordinary in today's culture, doesn't it? So, if you
do the math, you see that we had eleven people living in our house.

That is an important number to grasp in this story. Why?

Our house had *ten* beds.

That's right. Eleven people, ten beds. We were one bed short.

So I'm sure you're trying to figure out what the Slawek family did in order to solve this dilemma. Fortunately for us, we lived very close to my other grandmother's house, as well as lots of uncle and aunt's houses, filled with lots of my cousins, so more than likely someone was staying at our grandmother's or one of our cousin's house. Once it was time for bed at our house, if the beds were all filled up, we had the option to walk down the block or across the street and sleep at a relative's house. And, the worst case scenario, the last one home could always sleep on the couch in the living room of our house.

I can still recall the practical jokes I would pull on other members of my family, just to get a chance at sleeping in one of our beds. I have a particularly vivid recollection of waking up my sister Carol to tell her it was time for her to get out of bed and get started on her day. She would rub her eyes sleepily, but willingly comply with my request. What a cruel joke on my part—did I mention that I would wake Carol up, not at the normal early morning hour she needed—I would wake her up at *midnight*, just after I came home!

So when I say I learned at an early age to be grateful for my own bed to sleep in, you now know why that gratitude is well founded. And I know I speak for all the Slawek family when I offer up that statement of thanks.

Getting Practical: Naming Our Blessings

Since I'm big on gratitude, it shouldn't surprise you that my favorite holiday of the year is Thanksgiving. We always make a big deal of this all-American holiday.

One of the practical ways we engage in the practice of gratitude is by creating a document every year at our company that coincides with the Thanksgiving holiday. I like to refer to Thanksgiving as our high holiday here at FONA. We host a banquet every year where we bring in a speaker, usually a local pastor, to focus our attention on the true meaning of Thanksgiving. We have white tablecloths, an excellent meal, and we also use it as an occasion to pass out the end-of-the-year bonus checks—perfectly timed, preceding the Christmas shopping season. We have come to conclude that Thanksgiving really works well for us.

Now, back to the document we produce. We call the document *Thanksgiving: FONA Employee Accomplishments and Gratitude.* Within its pages, we invite our employees to focus their attention on what has taken place in the preceding year and articulate it.

To help them in this assignment, we give them topical guidelines they can choose to follow. They can write about areas such as:

- Significant team and personal achievements for which we give thanks.
- Meaningful events in our lives for which we are truly grateful.
- Cultural accomplishments for which we are grateful.
- Unique opportunities for which we are grateful.
- People in our lives for whom we are truly grateful.
- Other items for which we must give thanks.

Our employees may choose to follow that outline, or they can simply create a list of people and things for which to be grateful.

All the responses are put into a booklet, which is then printed up and given to everyone in the company. A recent Thanksgiving booklet included statements of thankfulness from employees like these:

"FONA's awesome benefits that help me sleep better at night."

"A place to call home."

"My wonderful, supportive and loving husband."

"Samantha Hawkins and Gina Acino, who never seem to run out of energy!"

"Learning, growing, and sharing life here at FONA with so many wonderful people who love what they do as much as I do."

Reading all these blessings from our employees, in every department from IT to the lab to the sales team, gave me great satisfaction. Not only have we created a company where there are so many good things, but we've raised the value of gratitude. It's a win-win.

As the CEO, it is my job to model the practice of gratitude from the top down, so I usually use the first page of the document to send my message to the company. Here's what I wrote for our Thanksgiving 2010 booklet:

Happy Thanksgiving 2010 from Joe Slawek!

Thanksgiving 2010 holds special significance for all of us here at FONA. There is much to be grateful for this year. FONA, along with each of us, has grown and prospered while we competed with the very best flavor companies in the world for the best customers in the world. Our commitment to Excellence has become increasingly evident and the professionalism of our people continues to grow throughout our organization. Our company has established a solid footing as a world-class flavor company in the eyes of our customers and our industry.

I am so very grateful to have the responsibility of serving our people, customers, and stakeholders every day. I am privileged to work with the very best people in our industry who relentlessly pursue excellence. I am grateful for so many things this year—I could write for days:

- *#1—Our wonderful people and new people.*
- *Our wonderful customers.*
- *Our wonderful Board of Advisors.*
- *Our excellent and continued growth of 16-17 percent so far.*
- *Our excellent audit scores.*
- *Our amazingly beautiful campus.*
- *Our extraordinary culture.*
- *The FONA Picnic.*
- *Inc. 5000's listing of fastest growing private companies.*
- *Being an Ernst and Young Entrepreneur of the Year® Award finalist.*
- *Our 2010 chaplains Bob and now Angel.*
- *Our FONA diversity.*
- *Our never-ending group of visitors.*
- *Our taste panels.*
- *The privilege of working with Luke as father and son.*
- *The Core Suppliers Program—they made us better.*

- *The reactor incident—it made us stronger and better.*
- *The safety and protection of our people.*
- *The clean results on over 700 products and 300 swabs—Wow!*
- *My wonderful family and their health and well-being.*
- *Family vacations TOGETHER!*
- *My salvation in my Lord and Savior, Jesus Christ.*
- *God's ever-present blessing, protection, and prosperity over FONA in these challenging economic times.*

I thank God for the many gifts, talents, events, responsibilities, authorities, successes, failures, problems, losses, gains, changes, weaknesses, and strengths which he gave us in the course of our development as a business. The credit for our success belongs to him for his abundant help, blessing, protection, mercy, and providence throughout our history, our today, and into our future. In turn, I seek first to honor him in all our activities.

Please make this Thanksgiving season a very special one at home and at FONA. Please be generous with your gratitude and appreciation. Be generous with your time and resources. Be generous with your forgiveness. Be generous with your kindness and goodwill. Be generous with your patience, love, hope, and joy, and most important, be selfless in order to be happiest.

With deep gratitude and indebtedness to each and all of you, Happy Thanksgiving, 2010!

—Joe Slawek

As you can see, this is not something that we just crank out with little thought. We give a great deal of time and attention to this booklet because it is a tangible example of how to put the discipline of gratitude into practice. Everybody is given the opportunity to contribute to this document and in 2010, we produced a booklet of standard paper size that contained thirty-three pages of gratitude!

I am grateful to God for all the lessons he has taught me in my personal life and in my role as a CEO. And when I say "all the lessons" I mean both the good ones and the ones that came as a result of difficult circumstances in life. It all works together and the result is something good. Our job is to ascertain what the lesson might be and how to benefit from it.

I'm grateful for what I learned from my parents and my siblings and my wife and my children. I'm grateful for what I learned as an eight year old delivering newspapers and then a ten year old collecting customers' money. I'm grateful for what I learned in my earliest days in the flavor industry. I'm grateful for the opportunity to work alongside so many wonderful people. I'm grateful for all the lessons I learned by launching out on my own and starting FONA. I'm grateful for the success we've achieved, the challenges we have addressed, and the brightness of our future. I'm grateful for flying and family and friends and church.

As the Apostle Paul wrote in his first letter to the church in Thessalonica: "Be thankful in all circumstances, for this is God's will for you who belong to Christ Jesus" (1 Thessalonians 5:18, NIV).

I've tried to apply the truth of this verse to my life, being thankful in every area. So I thank you, dear reader, for your willingness to trust me through these previous pages. I worked hard to stay faithful to the truths of God's Word, so it is in that vein that I can say to you with all confidence that you can trust what you have read here.

It's from God and it works. I know. I've trusted it and it's worked for me. Give it a try. You'll be glad you did.

Conclusion

It's early in the morning on a crisp February day. Here at FONA, it is the day set aside for the Monthly Employee Meeting. This month we have decided that the emphasis should be on our Core Values. All of our employees have gathered in our dining room for a ninety-minute slice of all that's going on at FONA.

As the staff gathers one can observe men and women of all ages, a variety of ethnicities, and a wide range of attire. Some are in jeans and sweaters, some wear white lab coats with the FONA logo embroidered in blue. Some are wearing hair nets, some are wearing hard hats, some are hatless. The warehouse guys are sporting their light blue shirts with the dark blue slacks. Some workers have surgical masks that rest around their necks, awaiting their position over their face when they get back to their work stations.

At precisely 7:30 the meeting begins with the Human Resources department introducing the new employees here at FONA. Hearty applause greets each new member of our team, as well as the applause given to the next group of people—those who are celebrating anniversaries with us as their employer. Today we are acknowledging folks who have been at FONA for one year, two years, three years, six years, and eight years. We have an employee celebrating ten years, which is quite special. Beyond applause, the happy team member is presented with a plaque and a check. In today's meeting we also acknowledge an employee with twelve years and another with fifteen years of service.

Our health insurance provider is here today for a brief presentation about some of the advantages and benefits of going with them as the provider. Once she has concluded her

PowerPoint presentation, it's time for the focus to turn toward core values.

In preparation for this morning's meeting, each of our seven core values have been placed one by one on seven tripods strategically located around the room. As our team sits in their seats, they are surrounded by the following seven reminders:

- Do the right thing.
- Be partner-centered.
- Relentlessly pursue excellence.
- Be a steward.
- Be generous.
- Pursue corporate excellence.
- Be forward-thinking.

What follows in the meeting is a series of five-minute presentations by our leadership team. Each will give a report of the status of their department, but today they will also highlight one of the core values as to how it relates to their particular area at FONA.

We begin with the report from Corporate Services. Corporate is doing well, we are told. Then, in the spirit of being generous, we hear about some of the important community service in which FONA is engaged.

Then we hear from Sales. Last month was a great month, we hear, but remember the core value of forward-thinking. Certainly it is good that last month was positive, but we want to anticipate what's ahead so we are always looking in that direction.

Next, we hear reports from four of our Business units: Grain,

Confections, Beverage, and Emerging. Each of those four areas gives us glimpses of their progress, but quickly turn the attention to how we are working on being partner-centered, relentlessly pursuing excellence, being a steward, and forward-thinking

These reports are followed by presentations from Operations and Tech Services. They follow the same model of reporting on their area, as well as creating the tie-in with one of our core values.

Once all the departments have reported, it is time for the CEO's Report, so I step to the front of the room and grab the microphone. You might not recognize me as the CEO by my appearance, since I make an effort to be one of the team, rather than standing out in some fancy coat and tie. Dressed in an oxford shirt and sweater vest (both with the FONA logo), I feel very comfortable surrounded by my team, and I hope they feel just as comfortable around me..

"One of our core values is to do the right thing," I begin, "and I think you all need to hear about how we as a company have stepped up to the plate in order to do just that very thing.

"You may have read in the newspaper or have seen it by driving by that one of our neighbors, a company called Aquascape, has experienced a crisis of major proportions. Because of all the snow that we've had this winter, a large portion of their roof has collapsed at their headquarters, and they are without a home right now.

"The President of Aquascape, Colleen Heitzler, as well as the owner, Greg Witt Stock, attend the same church Mary and I attend and this past weekend we were able to hear firsthand about the trial they are currently experiencing," I continued. I paused for a moment, then asked, "So what's the right thing to do in a situation like this one? To me, the answer is obvious. And that's why we invited Aquascape to set up their operations in our auditorium area until they can get back up on their feet."

With that comment, the room burst into an expected applause.

"We are not only doing what it right, but we're also extending generosity," I summarized. "And we are glad to do it. I realize that this decision affects all of you, so thank you for stepping up in order to show true hospitality and generosity."

At that point I invite Colleen to come up and say a few words and she steps forward without hesitation in order to express her heartfelt appreciation. "I don't know what we would look like right now if not for the generosity of FONA." She looks like she is working hard to hold back the tears, as the emotions run strong. "Thank you for turning your auditorium into a homeless shelter!"

I'm not a man who relishes public speaking opportunities, but I love to express my appreciation to my team. As the clock strikes nine I conclude with the truth from my heart:

It is a great time to be FONA!

And I believe that with all my heart. We have all come a long way and God isn't through with us yet. In many respects, perhaps the best is yet to come. I just want to be available to be used as a vessel, a servant, as God sees fit to use me.

I thought a final prayer would be a fitting way to close our time together.

My Prayer for Us and for You

Lord, thank you for letting me be Your Servant.

Lord, bless, protect, and prosper our people. Lord, please give your people, our leadership, our management, and our executives the wisdom, judgment, and courage to strategize, plan, and budget our business each year.

Lord, please guide our planning so as to fully care for your and our most important priority—our people.

Lord, we ask that you bring to mind those opportunities which will allow us to create industry leading growth, create profitability by doing only the necessary activities and eliminating unnecessary expenses, create an abundant and growing cash flow, implement succession plans for our wonderful people, provide technical and business breakthroughs, guide our international expansion, and improve our already excellent quality and services.

Lord, we acknowledge your ownership of all, and we express our dependence, indebtedness, and gratitude for all you have done for us. Lord, we ask you to counsel us on the detailed operation of your business.

Lord, we pray this prayer in the name of Jesus Christ. Amen. Amen. Amen.

APPENDIX

The Vision at FONA

FONA is the leader in the flavor industry acknowledged for our relentless pursuit of excellence that translates to customer growth, employee growth, and business growth. We will be the chosen and preferred partner for our target customers and markets and will earn this distinction through our industry-leading customer collaboration, support, and focus. The FONA brand will be synonymous with EXCELLENCE, as conveyed in each and every experience. The FONA brand will be synonymous with technical and business innovation and industry-leading business models.

The Mission at FONA

FONA grows and connects our people, our customers, our brands, our businesses, and our communities through our commitment to GROWTH and EXCELLENCE. We are focused on delivering high-value taste, technology, and manufacturing solutions that grow consumer acceptance, brand preference, and loyalty for our target customers in the areas of Confection, Grain, Beverage, Performance Nutrition, OTC, and Emerging. We endeavor to establish high-touch, collaborative, integrated partnerships with "willing, able, and growing" customers through our solution-focused business units, strategic platforms, and world-class sales team. Our strategic focus is to support our customers internationally while also proactively pursuing select opportunities where we can duplicate our value and success. We accomplish this through the establishment of a culture that is centered around timeless core values, is committed to EXCELLENCE, identifies and strives to apply the best management practices, and processes and hires and develops world class talent. This winning approach fuels our consistent high growth and creates the profitability necessary to fund our continued expansion.

The Values at FONA

FONA's culture can be described as partner-centered, growth-oriented, positive, and dynamic. We attract employees who are willing, able, and committed to personal and professional growth. Our belief is that all people have innate value and significance and are worthy of dignity and respect. We seek to create and sustain an open environment that is palpably inclusive, values diversity, promotes innovation, and provides growth opportunities for ALL FONA team members. We are committed to the highest standards of ethical and moral conduct as we manage and grow our business. Our core values are best expressed in the following seven statements:

- *To do the right thing for all stakeholders in all situations.*
  This means we are upfront and honest, always practicing mutual respect. We exceed compliance expectations of our customers, regulatory bodies, and government entities. We aspire to involve wide groups in key decisions, and ensure that everyone feels as though they contribute to the process. Our behavior is exemplary in integrity, tolerance, and honesty. We maintain a family-first environment where employees can provide for the needs of their loved ones and be a part of enjoying the fruits of their labor.

- *To demonstrate a relentless, passionate partner-centricity.*
  Our business model is built around finding compelling, unique solutions for our partner's greatest business challenges. We believe there is an important distinction between customers and

partners. Customers look for concrete selection criteria, which can be objectified and researched; partners seek mutually-beneficial, long-term relationships based on trust and solutions well beyond the simple criteria. We are entrepreneurial, passionate, and focused in delighting our partners. We believe that all parties make an impact on our business success. We over-invest to understand partner needs. We have and will deliberately build reserve capacity to meet unspoken demand, and thus, are ready for our partners to succeed with us. We listen for our partner feedback and act upon their insights.

- *To establish and nurture a high-performance work environment.* We compete in an extremely dynamic industry against powerful, resilient competitors. Our primary competitive advantage is our people—our drive, passion, intelligence, and talent. We recruit, select, and equip best-in-class talent in order to win. We provide generous rewards to key financial contributors. We are a non-elitist meritocracy, where the best ideas from dedicated contributors are recognized and rewarded. We expect a great deal from every FONA team member as we continually pursue excellence in our high-performance work environment. We believe that succession management is critical to sustain our organizational performance.

- *To effectively steward our resources and opportunities.* Optimizing our organization requires a disciplined, balanced emphasis on strategy, financial performance, and personal accountability. Excellence is imbedded in all of our activities, from technology and innovation through flavor delivery and logistics. We create strategic commitments in our business units where well-researched strategies and plans are developed and executed. We steward our resources—people, finances, facility—incredibly well. We opportunistically seize business opportunities that others neglect. We believe empowerment and alignment releases potential in people and organizations.

- *To invest consistently and effectively in our growth and innovation.* FONA is a learning organization. Our investments in development and growth of our people yield a sustained return in our flexibility, innovation, and resilience. The people of FONA are future-oriented—we continue to invest in ourselves and in our business because we believe that "our best work is ahead of us." We encourage experimentation (and thus accept setbacks and failure). We invest in our people to stimulate growth and innovation. We take feedback seriously, and we examine our problems realistically and build capabilities and capacities to address our weaknesses. We establish structures and practices that encourage people to provide feedback to each other and invest in one another.

- *To share generously with our people and community.* The people of FONA display incredible amounts of warmth and regard for each other. We bring individual contributors together into a workplace community where the individual experiences respect and care. Our employee benefits are among the richest in the industry, reflecting our belief that if you take good care of your people, they will take good care of your customers and the business. We strive to balance short-term care of our employees with enabling opportunities for their long-term growth. We recognize that we do not exist for ourselves; FONA makes a vital and necessary contribution to our larger communities and our industry communities.

- *To outperform our industry in pursuit of profitable growth.* Financial performance allows us to "control our own destiny" in remaining independent and rewarding our stakeholders. We believe that growth is simply the "applause" of customers for delivering excellence on every project and opportunity. We provide the tools for financial performance to our employees— enabling each individual to make line-of-sight contributions to the fiscal health of our organization. We demonstrate fiscal responsibility in our expense management—spending FONA resources as though they were our own. And our business strategy has been articulated so that our financial priorities are clearly understood by all team members.

Made in United States
Orlando, FL
13 January 2023

28627165R00072